Essential Keto Bread cookbook

50 Easy Keto Bread Recipes for Effortless Baking in Your Bread Maker, Low-Carb Bread

By

MARK ANTHONY

CONTENTS

INTRODUCTION 6

What Is Keto Bread? 8

Keto Bread Recipe 10

    Paleo Gluten-Free Low Carb English Muffin Recipe in a Minute 10

    Low Carb Gluten Free Cranberry Bread 13

    Low Sugar Gluten Free Pumpkin Bread 16

    Keto Macadamia Bread 19

    Garlic & Herb Focaccia 22

    Gluten Free & Keto Pizza Crust 26

    Keto + Low Carb Cornbread Muffins 30

    Low Carb Chelsea Buns 33

    Sweet Keto Challah Bread Recipe 37

    Nut-Free Keto Buns 40

    Low Carb Carrot Cake Muffins 45

    Keto Zucchini Bread 48

    Jalapeno Low Carb Bagel 51

    Cheesy Skillet Bread 54

    Paleo Chocolate Zucchini Bread 57

    Keto Fiber Bread Rolls Recipe 62

    3 Ingredient Paleo Naan 65

    Keto Fathead Bagels 68

Cheesy Keto Garlic Bread - using mozzarella dough 71
Low Carb Asparagus Egg Bites 74
Keto Cream Cheese Bread 77
Cheddar Garlic Fathead Rolls 81
Healthy 3 Ingredient Mini Paleo Pizza Bases Crusts 85
Low Carb Blueberry English Muffin Bread Loaf 89
Parmesan & Tomato Keto Bread Buns 91
Gluten Free, Paleo & Keto Drop Biscuits 95
Buttery Low Carb Flatbread 99
Low Carb Paleo Tortillas Recipe 102
3 Minute Low Carb Biscuits 106
Keto Banana Bread 108
Hot Ham and Cheese Roll-Ups with Dijon Butter Glaze 112
Sunflower Pumpkin Seed Psyllium Bread 116
Rosemary and Garlic Coconut Flour Bread 119
Keto Paleo Low-Carb Stuffing 122
15-Minute Gluten Free, Low Carb & Keto Tortillas 126
Coconut Flour Mini Cheese Loaves 130
Coconut Flour Psyllium Husk Bread – Paleo 133
Cauliflower Tortillas 136

Rosemary Olive Bread 139

Wholemeal Seed & Grain Apricot Loaf by Allinson's 142

Keto Cheddar Jalapeño "Cornbread" 145

Rosemary and Garlic Coconut Flour Bread 148

Easy Keto Zucchini Bread Recipe with Bacon and Cheese 151

Keto Jalapeño Cheese Bread 154

Keto Cloud Bread ("Oopsie Bread") 157

Everything Keto Rolls 160

Keto Low Carb Banana Bread Recipe with Almond Flour 163

Keto Spinach Dip Stuffed Bread 167

Cheesy Keto Hamburger Buns 171

Zucchini Coconut Bread 173

CONCLUSION 176

INTRODUCTION

You don't have to give up bread when you go on the keto diet. Nor do you have to be stuck with spongy store-bought breads. The healthy recipes in this book have been selected specially to take care of your bread loaves, rolls, buns and bagels needs while
on the keto diet. Additionally, a number of recipes are also provided for pizza dough, flatbread, tortillas and muffins.

No matter the type of bread you love, you will find several recipes that will meet your needs in this collection. Some like bread fluffy while others prefer chewy, but everyone wants delicious bread. The creative combination of keto approved ingredients produce hearty and flavorful bread with a delicious crust. Bread slices have never been more delicious when toasted
up for breakfast!
Coconut and almond combine beautifully in the Coconut Almond Bread recipe to give you a flufiy loaf with a nutty flavor.
lather on maple syrup or butter on the mouthwatering slices of the Coconut Herb Bread and you won't want to stop eating. You
will never have enough of the warm and delicious Easy Keto

Rolls. Variations of the keto diet are also taken into consideration: Vegetarian and vegans will find many diary free recipes that are not only suitable for them but also delicious too.

A good number of the recipes are also suitable for gluten free and paleo diet adherents.

Keto bread recipes are not only for breakfast. They come in handy as side dishes and are very useful for scooping up soups or

stews. Why order lunch at work when you can easily make it at home and take it with you. The Flatbread and Tortilla categories

give you several options for making wraps and sandwiches. All you need is to throw together some cooked meat and vegetables

with your favorite toppings.

You don't need a bread machine to make any of these recipes. A simple stand or hand-held mixer and an oven are all that are required, They are easy to make and your family and guests will be impressed. The few preparation steps are also clearly written and can be followed by anyone no matter their level of cooking or baking experience. They are quick to make, keto approved and very nutritious.

Enjoy and stay healthy!

WHAT IS KETO BREAD?

You may have heard of the newest keto diet trend, keto bread. Simply put, this is bread that theoretically fits into a keto diet. When added carefully, keto bread can be incorporated into a ketogenic diet. Typically low calorie — one popular brand, Franz Keto, contains only 40 calories a slice per its white bread — keto bread is also typically lower in carbohydrates and higher in protein and fiber than other breads.

A slice of Frank Keto White, for example, contains 12 grams carbs — all of which are fiber — and 4 grams protein per slice. This is due to the bread's ingredients, which contain wheat gluten (a form of protein) and inulin or chicory root fiber. A slice of typical white bread, on the other hand, contains 75 calories, 14 grams carbs, 1 gram fiber, and 2 grams protein, per the USDA database.

The major plus of keto bread: It allows keto dieters to eat bread. For keto dieters, bread and bagels are typically off limits. We're now seeing an explosion in keto-friendly product innovation, where popular carb-rich foods are substituted for low-carb alternatives. Bread is undoubtedly one of those foods, giving people the option to enjoy their favorite foods, not feel deprived, and still meet their carb budget.

How to Eat Bread on the Keto Diet

If you follow the keto diet, you have a very strict carbohydrate limit to adhere to — and depending on what else you eat in a day, you may only be able to enjoy an open-faced sandwich. People eating keto breads should keep in mind that the Nutrition Info apply to one serving, usually one slice.

And some keto breads are high in saturated fat. Some brands include plenty of saturated fats, which is correlated with heart disease. The Keto Thin Bread from Julian Bakery, for instance, contains 5 grams saturated fat per slice.

One more potential drawback: Keto breads may not be as rich in other nutrients that are found in whole grains, such as B vitamins and minerals.

Keto Bread Recipe

PALEO GLUTEN-FREE LOW CARB ENGLISH MUFFIN RECIPE IN A MINUTE

A paleo low carb English muffin recipe that's soft and buttery inside, crusty on the outside. These gluten-free English muffins are easy to make in 2 minutes, with 5 ingredients!

Prep Time 2 minutes
Cook Time 3 minutes
Total Time 5 minutes

Ingredients

- 1 tbsp Butter (or ghee, or coconut oil)
- 1 large Egg (or equivalent egg whites)
- 3 tbsp Blanched almond flour
- 1/2 tbsp Coconut flour
- 1 pinch Sea salt
- 1/2 tsp Gluten-free baking powder

Instructions

- Melt ghee (or butter) in a microwave or oven safe ramekin or other container, about 4 in (10 cm) diameter with a flat bottom. This takes about 30 seconds. (If using the oven only, you can melt it in the oven while it preheats. Remove once melted.)
- Add the remaining ingredients and stir until well combined. Let sit for a minute to allow the mixture to thicken.
- Microwave method: Microwave for about 90 seconds, until firm.

- ➢ Oven method: Bake for about 15 minutes at 350 degrees F (177 degrees C), until the top is firm and spring-y to the touch.

- ➢ Run a knife along the edge and flip over a plate to release. Slice in half, then toast in the toaster.

Recipe Notes

- If you prefer more/smaller slices, you can also make it in a mug instead of a ramekin, then just pop those in the toaster in batches.

Serving size: 2 large slices (entire recipe)

Nutrition Info

Calories 307
Fat 27g
Protein 12g
Total Carbs 8g
Net Carbs 4g
Fiber 4g
Sugar 2g

LOW CARB GLUTEN FREE CRANBERRY BREAD

A delicious gluten free low carb cranberry bread with fresh cranberries. This sugar-free bread uses a combination of stevia and erythritol sweeteners.

Prep Time 10 minutes
Cook Time 1 hour 15 minutes
Total Time 1 hour 25 minutes
Servings 12 people

Ingredients

- 1/2 teaspoon Steviva stevia powder
- 1 1/2 teaspoons baking powder
- 1 teaspoon blackstrap molasses optional (for brown sugar flavor)
- 4 large eggs at room temperature
- 1/2 cup coconut milk
- 1/2 teaspoon baking soda
- 2 cups almond flour
- 1/2 cup powdered erythritol or Swerve,
- 1 teaspoon salt
- 4 tablespoons unsalted butter melted (or coconut oil)
- 1 bag cranberries 12 ounces

Instructions

- Preheat oven to 350 degrees; grease a 9-by-5 inch loaf pan and set aside.
- In a large bowl, whisk together flour, erythritol, stevia, baking powder, baking soda, and salt; set aside.
- In a medium bowl, combine butter, molasses, eggs, and coconut milk.
- Mix dry mixture into wet mixture until well combined.
- Fold in cranberries. Pour batter into prepared pan.

- Bake until a toothpick inserted in the center of the loaf comes clean, about 1 hour and 15 minutes.
- Transfer pan to a wire rack; let bread cool 15 minutes before removing from pan.

Nutrition Info

Calories 179 Calories from Fat 135

Total Fat 15g 23%

Saturated Fat 4g 20%

Cholesterol 72mg 24%

Sodium 276mg 12%

Potassium 38mg 1%

Total Carbohydrates 7g 2%

Dietary Fiber 2g 8%

Sugars 1g

Protein 6.4g 13%

LOW SUGAR GLUTEN FREE PUMPKIN BREAD

A moist low sugar, low carb, and gluten free coconut flour pumpkin bread with no added sugars, and a delicious blend of spices to bring out the pumpkin flavor.

Prep time: 10 mins
Cook time: 60 mins
Total time: 1 hour 10 mins

Ingredients

- 1 cup coconut flour
- ½ tsp salt
- 1 tsp Sweetleaf Stevia
- 2 tsp cinnamon
- ½ tsp ginger
- 1 tsp ground cloves
- ½ cup Swerve Sweetener, granulated
- 8 eggs (I used large)
- 1 tsp baking soda
- ½ tsp baking powder
- 2 tbsp vanilla extract
- 1 stick butter
- 1, 15-oz can of pureed Pumpkin

Instructions

- Preheat oven to 350 degrees F, and grease a 9x5 bread pan with butter. (Using oil or butter vs spray helps the bread not to stick to the pan.)
- In a large bowl, mix together the dry ingredients of coconut flour, Swerve Sweetener, baking soda, baking powder, salt, Sweetleaf Stevia, cinnamon, ginger and ground cloves.

- In another bowl, mix together the wet ingredients. When well mixed, add the wet ingredients into the large ingredients and whisk well. (If using a blender, a low-medium blend is fine.)
- Fill the 9x5 bread pan with the pumpkin bread, and bake in the oven until a tooth pick comes out clear. For me, the 50-1 hr mark was perfect.

KETO MACADAMIA BREAD

Prep Time: 15 minutes

Cook Time: 45 minutes

Serving: 8

Ingredients

- ❖ 2 scoops grass-fed whey protein powder
- ❖ 2 tbsp ground flax seeds
- ❖ 1 tsp baking soda
- ❖ 1 cup macadamia nuts
- ❖ 1/4 cup almond flour
- ❖ 3/4 tsp himalayan salt

- ❖ 4 eggs
- ❖ 2 egg whites
- ❖ 1/4 cup grass-fed ghee, melted
- ❖ 1 tbsp apple cider vinegar

Instructions

- ➢ Preheat the oven to 350 F. Rub the bottom of your loaf pan with ghee or extra virgin olive oil to prevent sticking.
- ➢ In a food processor, pulse the macadamia nuts for about 30-45 seconds or until it creates a flour consistency.
- ➢ Add the almond flour, whey protein, flax seeds, baking soda, and himalayan salt to the food processor. Continue to pulse until ingredients are mixed well.
- ➢ In a medium size bowl beat eggs, egg whites, melted ghee and apple cider vinegar with a whisk.
- ➢ Fold in dry ingredients.
- ➢ Pour into a greased loaf pan and bake for approximately 45 minutes.

Nutrition Info

Calories: 262

Fat: 23g

Carbs: 4g

Protein: 12g

Fiber: 2g

Sugar: 1g (added sugar: 0g)

Sodium: 417mg

GARLIC & HERB FOCACCIA

Quit bread for good and get this grain free focaccia on your plate.

Prep time 10 mins
Cook time 20 mins
Total time 30 mins
Serves: 8 slices

Ingredients

Dry Ingredients

- ½ tsp Xanthan Gum
- 1 tsp Garlic Powder
- 1 tsp Flaky Salt
- 1 cup Almond Flour
- ¼ cup Coconut Flour
- ½ tsp Baking Soda
- ½ tsp Baking Powder

Wet Ingredients

- 2 eggs
- 1 tbsp Lemon Juice
- 2 tsp Olive oil + 2 tbsp Olive Oil to drizzle

Top with Italian Seasoning and TONS of flaky salt!

Instructions

- Heat oven to 350 and line a baking tray or 8-inch round pan with parchment.

- Whisk together the dry ingredients making sure there are no lumps.
- Beat the egg, lemon juice, and oil until combined.
- Mix the wet and the dry together, working quickly, and scoop the dough into your pan.
- ***Make sure not to mix the wet and dry until you are ready to put the bread in the oven because the leavening reaction begins once it is mixed!!!
- Smooth the top and edges with a spatula dipped in water (or your hands) then use your finger to dimple the dough. Don't be afraid to go deep on the dimples! Again, a little water keeps it from sticking.
- Bake covered for about 10 minutes. Drizzle with Olive Oil bake for an additional 10-15 minutes uncovering to brown gently.
- Top with more flaky salt, olive oil (optional), a dash of Italian seasoning and fresh basil. Let cool completely before slicing for optimal texture!!
- You can also cut it into squares and you'd just want to adjust how many servings you get vs the macros1

Nutrition Info

Calories: 166

Fat: 13

Carbohydrates: 7

Fiber: 4

Protein: 7

GLUTEN FREE & KETO PIZZA CRUST

Looking for a quick and easy keto pizza? This (15-minute!!) gluten free, dairy free and keto stove top pizza crust is most definitely for you!

Prep Time: 10 minutes
Cook Time: 5 minutes
Total Time: 15 minutes
Servings: slices

Ingredients

For the keto pizza dough:

- 24 g coconut flour
- 2 teaspoons xanthan gum
- 2 teaspoons baking powder
- 2 teaspoons apple cider vinegar
- 1 egg lightly beaten
- 5 teaspoons water as needed
- 1/4 teaspoon kosher salt depending on whether sweet or savory
- 96 g almond flour

Topping suggestions:

- mozzarella cheese
- our keto marinara sauce
- pepperoni or salami
- fresh basil

Instructions

For the keto dough:

- Add almond flour, coconut flour, xanthan gum, baking powder and salt to food processor. Pulse until thoroughly combined.
- Pour in apple cider vinegar with the food processor running. Once it has distributed evenly, pour in the egg. Followed by the water, adding just enough for it to come together into a ball. The dough will be sticky to touch from the xanthan gum, but still sturdy.
- Wrap dough in plastic wrap and knead it through the plastic for a minute or two. Think of it a bit like a stress ball. The dough should be smooth and not significantly cracked (a couple here and there are fine). In which case get it back to the food processor and add in more water 1 teaspoon at a time. Allow dough to rest for 10 minutes at room temperature (and up to 5 days in the fridge).
- If cooking on the stove top: heat up a skillet or pan over medium/high heat while your dough rests (you want the pan to be very hot!). If using the oven: heat up a pizza stone, skillet or baking tray in the oven at 350°F/180°C. The premise is that you need to blind cook/bake the crust first on both sides without toppings on a very hot surface.
- Roll out dough between two sheets of parchment paper with a rolling pin. You can play with thickness here, but

we like to roll it out nice and thin (roughly 12 inches in diameter) and fold over the edges (pressing down with wet fingertips).
- Cook the pizza crust in your pre-heated skillet or pan, top-side down first, until blistered (about 2 minutes, depending on your skillet and heat). Lower heat to medium/low, flip over your pizza crust, add toppings of choice and cover with a lid. Alternatively you can always transfer it to your oven on grill to finish off the pizza.
- Serve right away. Alternatively, note that the dough can be kept in the fridge for about 5 days. So you can make individual mini pizzettes throughout the week.

Nutrition Info

Calories 118 Calories from Fat 81

Total Fat 9g 14%

Saturated Fat 1.3g 7%

Cholesterol 27mg 9%

Sodium 116mg 5%

Potassium 10mg 0%

Total Carbohydrates 5.5g 2%

Dietary Fiber 3g 12%

Sugars 0.8g

Protein 5g 10%

KETO + LOW CARB CORNBREAD MUFFINS

These muffins are completely corn-free, but they are reminiscent of real cornbread muffins without the high carb count. They're perfect as a side, breakfast, or snack!

Prep Time: 15 minutes
Cook Time: 25 minutes
Total Time: 40 minutes
Servings: 12

Ingredients

- 3 eggs, slightly beaten
- 1 cup (128g) coconut flour

- 1/4 cup (30g) almond meal
- 1/2 cup heavy whipping cream
- 1/2 cup unsweetened coconut milk (from a carton, not a jar)
- 5 tbsp salted butter, melted
- 3 oz cream cheese, softened
- 3 tbsp (27g) Swerve Confectioners
- 1 1/2 tsp baking powder
- 1/8 tsp salt

Instructions

- Pre-heat oven to 350 F.
- If you're using a silicone muffin pan like I did, you don't need to grease the pan. However, if you're not using silicone, I recommend lightly greasing it or using liners for easy removal.
- In a large bowl, combine eggs, heavy whipping cream, coconut milk, melted butter (cooled slightly), and cream cheese. Using a hand mixer, mix everything until the cream cheese is well-incorporated. (It's okay if you have a few small flecks remaining.) Set aside.
- In a medium-sized bowl, combine coconut flour, almond meal, Swerve Confectioners, baking powder, and salt. Mix thoroughly.

- ➢ Add dry ingredients to wet and mix thoroughly using your hand mixer.
- ➢ Evenly distribute the batter across the holes, pressing the batter down a bit with the back of a spoon. (The batter is thick and easily forms pockets.) They will be about 80% full.
- ➢ Place in the oven and bake for 20-25 minutes until the edges start to brown and an inserted toothpick comes out mostly clean. Do not overbake. The center should still be slightly soft (but not uncooked) when you pull the pan out of the oven.
- ➢ Cool and enjoy!

Nutrition Info

Calories 169 Calories from Fat 126

Total Fat 14g 22%

Saturated Fat 8g 40%

Cholesterol 64mg 21%

Sodium 105mg 4%

Potassium 105mg 3%

Total Carbohydrates 7.8g 3%

Dietary Fiber 3.7g 15%

Sugars 0g

Protein 4g 8%

LOW CARB CHELSEA BUNS

Low-carb Chelsea buns are so light and fluffy, who knew they could be this easy to make (and enjoy).

Prep Time 15 mins
Cook Time 20 mins
Total Time 35 mins
Servings: 4

Ingredients

- 5 tbsp granulated sweetener of choice or more, to your taste
- 4 egg whites
- 200 g almond meal/flour
- 40 g psyllium husk
- 2 tsp baking powder
- 1 tsp vanilla
- 250 ml boiling water

Cinnamon filling

- 2 tsp ground cinnamon
- 2 tsp granulated sweetener of choice
- lemon zest optional

Glaze

- 4 tbsp powdered sweetener
- 1 tsp vanilla optional
- water enough to make a liquid glaze

Instructions

Low Carb Chelsea Bun Dough

- ➤ Place all the dry ingredients together in a bowl and mix well.
- ➤ Make a hole in the middle of the dry ingredients and add the egg whites and vanilla. Mix just a little so you can't see the egg whites any more.
- ➤ Add 1/3 the boiling water gently and slowly, mix. Add another 1/3, mix. Add the final 1/3 and mix until it looks like a sticky dough.
- ➤ If the dough looks too wet, add an extra tablespoon of psyllium husk, if too dry, add a teaspoon of water at a time.
- ➤ Pour the dough onto a large sheet of baking parchment/paper. Place another piece of baking parchment/paper on top.
- ➤ Press out with your hands until it is a rectangle shape and 1cm / 1/2 inch thick.

Cinnamon filling

- ➤ Mix the cinnamon and sweetener together and sprinkle all over the rolled dough.

- Using the baking parchment/paper, start to roll the dough up along the longest side.
- Continue to roll it into one long roll, then cut into even slices.
- Place each slice in a ring tin that has been oiled and lined.
- Bake at 180C/350F for 20-30 minutes, or until golden, and baked in the centre of each Chelsea bun.

Glaze

- Mix the powdered sweetener, vanilla and water together to make a liquid glaze.
- Drizzle, pour or spoon all over.
- Enjoy warm or cold.

Nutrition Info

Calories 246 Calories from Fat 167

Total Fat 18.6g 29%

Total Carbohydrates 13.7g 5%

Dietary Fiber 8.2g 33%

Sugars 1.6g

Protein 10g

SWEET KETO CHALLAH BREAD RECIPE

Sweet Keto Challah Bread Recipe (Braided) is made into perfection without Flour, perfect for Low Carb option.

Prep Time 10 minutes
Cook Time 45 minutes
Total Time 55 minutes
20 Serving

Ingredients

- ❖ 4 Eggs

- 50g (1/4 Cup)Oil
- 1 Cup (100g) Unflavored Protein
- 2/3 Cup (85g) Vanilla Protein
- 1/2 tsp salt
- 50g (1/3 Cup)Sukrin Plus
- 345g (1,5 Cup) Cream Cheese
- 60g (1/4 Cup)Butter
- 60g (1/4 Cup)Heavy Cream
- 1/3 tsp (3g) Baking Soda
- 2 1/2 tsp (12g) Baking Powder
- 1 tsp (4g) Xanthan
- 1/2 of Lemon Zest
- 1/4 Cup (30g) Dried Berries (I have used cranberries)

Instructions

- Heat up the oven to 160C or 320F
- In a separate bowl, mix eggs into fluffiness, then add sugar substitute and mix again.
- Add Cream Cheese and all of the liquid ingredients and mix again
- Once that is properly mixed, add all of the dried ingredients and finish it with mixing it all together.
- Take it our of the mixer and add fresh lemon zest followed by dry cranberries

- ➢ Gently hand mix it into the dough, which is then poured into a silicone baking pan, depending on your desired shape.
- ➢ Bake for 45 Min
- ➢ Bon appetite

Nutrition Info

Calories: 158

Total Fat: 13g

Saturated Fat: 6g

Trans Fat: 0g

Unsaturated Fat: 6g

Cholesterol: 66mg

Sodium: 241mg

Carbohydrates: 2g

Protein: 9g

NUT-FREE KETO BUNS

Hands-on 10-15 minutes

Overall 1 hour 15 minutes

Serving: 10 buns

Ingredients

Dry ingredients

- ❖ 1 1/4 cup fine defatted sesame seed flour (100 g / 3.5 oz)
- ❖ 2/3 cup flaxmeal (100 g / 3.5 oz)
- ❖ 2/3 cup coconut flour (80 g / 2.8 oz)
- ❖ 1/3 packed cup psyllium husk powder (40 g / 1.4 oz)
- ❖ 2 tsp garlic powder
- ❖ 2 tsp onion powder
- ❖ 2 tsp cream of tartar or apple cider vinegar
- ❖ 1 tsp baking soda
- ❖ 1 tsp salt (pink Himalayan or sea salt)
- ❖ 5 tbsp sesame seeds (or sunflower, flax, poppy seeds) or 1-2 tbsp caraway seeds for topping

Wet ingredients

- ❖ 6 large egg whites
- ❖ 2 large eggs
- ❖ 2 1/4 - 2 1/2 cups water depending on the consistency, boiling or lukewarm depending on the method - see intro (540 ml / 18 fl oz) - Use only 2 cups if using ground sesame seeds / sesame seed meal instead of defatted sesame seed flour.

Instructions

- Preheat the oven to 175 °C/ 350 °F. Use a kitchen scale to measure all the ingredients carefully. I used defatted sesame seed flour but you can try sesame seed meal instead and use less water. To make sesame seed meal, I just blend the seeds until powdered (just like I do with flax seeds to make flax meal).
- I used Sukrin sesame flour (UK) but you can use this brand too (US) - both should be defatted. Nut-Free Keto Buns
- Mix all the dry ingredients apart from the seeds for the topping in a bowl: sesame flour, coconut flour, flaxmeal, psyllium powder, ...
- Do not use whole psyllium husks - if you cannot find psyllium husk powder, use a blender or coffee grinder and process until fine. If you get already prepared psyllium husk powder, remember to weigh it before adding to the recipe. I used whole psyllium husks which I grinded myself. Do not use just measure cups - different products have different weights per cup! Nut-Free
- ..., baking soda, cream of tartar, garlic powder, ...
- Cream of tartar and baking soda act as leavening agents. This is how it works: To get 2 teaspoons of gluten-free

baking powder, you need 1/2 a teaspoon of baking soda and 1 teaspoon of cream of tartar (double in this recipe of 10 buns). If you don't have cream of tartar, instead you can use apple cider vinegar and add it to the wet ingredients. Nut-Free Keto Buns

- ... onion powder and salt
- Add the egg whites and eggs and process well using a mixer until the dough is thick.
- Nut-Free Keto Buns The reason you shouldn't use only whole eggs is that the buns wouldn't rise with so many egg yolks in. Don't waste them - use them for making Home-made Mayo, Easy Hollandaise Sauce or Lemon Curd.
- Add boiling water and mix until well combined. Nut-Free Keto Buns
- Using a spoon or hands, form the buns and place them on a non-stick baking tray or a parchment paper. They will grow in size as they bake, so make sure to leave some space between them. Top each of the buns with sesame seeds (or any other seeds) and press them into the dough, so they don't fall out.
- Place in the oven and cook for 55-60 minutes. Remove from the oven, let the tray cool down and place the buns on a rack to cool down to room temperature. Store them

at room temperature if you plan to use them in the next couple of days or in the freezer for future use.
- ➢ Top with butter or cream cheese, burger meat and meat-free toppings. Enjoy!

Nutrition Info

Net carbs 3.5 grams
Protein 12.3 grams
Fat 10.6 grams
Calories 180 kcal

LOW CARB CARROT CAKE MUFFINS

This low carb carrot cake muffins are great for snacking! Sugar free, gluten free, and keto recipe.

Prep Time: 10 minutes
Cook Time: 25 minutes
Cooling Time: 5 minutes
Total Time: 35 minutes
Servings: 6

Ingredients

- 1 carrot peeled and grated
- 1 cup almond flour
- 3 eggs
- ¼ cup melted butter
- 2 tbs low carb sweetener eg Swerve
- ½ tsp baking powder
- ½ tsp vanilla extract

Instructions

- Preheat the oven to 350F (175C).
- In a stand mixer bowl, add almond flour, eggs, melted butter, sweetener, baking powder and vanilla extract. Blend until fully combined.
- Stir in the grated carrot until mixed through the batter.
- Divide the mixture between a six-hole muffin pan that has been lined with paper or silicone liners.
- Bake in a preheated oven for 20-25 minutes or until cooked through. Let cool for 5 minutes before serving.

Nutrition Info

Calories 210 Calories from Fat 171

Total Fat 19g 29%

Saturated Fat 6g 30%

Cholesterol 102mg 34%

Sodium 105mg 4%

Potassium 102mg 3%

Total Carbohydrates 5g 2%

Dietary Fiber 2g 8%

Sugars 1g

Protein 6g 12%

KETO ZUCCHINI BREAD

A delicious Keto Zucchini Bread that goes perfectly with grass-fed butter - and is a great way to use up all that extra zucchini from the garden!

Prep Time 20 minutes
Cook Time 1 hour
Total Time 1 hour 20 minutes
Serving: 8 servings

Ingredients

- ½ cup butter, softened
- ¼ cup Allulose
- ¼ cup Lakanto Granular Sweetener
- 3 Eggs
- 2 cups Almond Flour
- ½ cup Coconut Flour
- 1 ½ cups Grated Zucchini (approx. 1 medium zucchini)
- 1 tsp. Baking Soda
- 1 tsp. Baking Powder
- 2 tsp. Cinnamon
- 1 tsp. Ginger
- ½ tsp. Xanthan Gum

Instructions

- Preheat oven to 325. Grease a loaf pan with coconut or avocado oil cooking spray and set aside.
- In a large mixing bowl, cream together the butter, allulose, and lakanto sweetener until light and fluffy.
- Add in the eggs, one at a time, beating until combined, then stir in the grated zucchini.

- ➢ Dump the almond flour, coconut flour, baking soda, baking powder, cinnamon, ginger, and xanthan gum on top of the wet ingredients, then mix well.
- ➢ Scoopthe batter into the loaf pan (It will most likely be thick) and spread out evenly.
- ➢ Bake at 325 for 50-60 minutes, until set in the center. Remove from the oven and let sit in the loaf pan until completely cool - and be sure to keep an eye on your dog!
- ➢ Enjoy with butter, my favorite topping.

Nutrition Info

Calories: 317

Total Fat: 28g

Carbohydrates: 8g

Fiber: 4g

Protein: 8g

JALAPENO LOW CARB BAGEL

Prep Time: 10 minutes
Cook Time: 30 minutes
Total Time: 40 minutes
Servings: 6 Bagels
Calories: 273kcal

Ingredients

- ❖ 2 cups Mozzarella cheese grated
- ❖ 2 oz Cream cheese
- ❖ 1 cup Almond flour
- ❖ 1 teaspoon baking powder

- ❖ 3 Jalapeno peppers
- ❖ 2 Eggs
- ❖ 1 oz Cheddar cheese grated

Instructions

- ➢ Preheat the oven to 200C/400F
- ➢ Chop and deseed the jalapeno peppers. Slice a few thin circles and set them aside for the decoration.
- ➢ In a bowl, mix the almond flour and baking powder.
- ➢ Add the chopped jalapeno peppers and eggs. Mix well.
- ➢ In another bowl add the mozzarella and cream cheese.
- ➢ Cook in the microwave for 2 minutes, stopping after 1 minute to give it a gentle stir (you'll end up with crispy bits around the bowl otherwise).
- ➢ Remove and stir, then add in the almond flour mixture.
- ➢ Stir well and combine until you have a blended dough.
- ➢ Break the dough up into 6 pieces and roll out the pieces to make into a bagel shape OR use a donut tray to place the dough in. (I find this easier to keep them neater).
- ➢ Decorate the bagels with sliced jalapenos and sprinkle with some grated Cheddar cheese.
- ➢ Bake for 20-30 minutes, keeping an eye on them that they bake until golden.
- ➢ Eat and enjoy!

Nutrition Info

273 Calories

22g Fat

16g Protein

6g Total Carb

2g Fibre

4g Net Carbs

CHEESY SKILLET BREAD

Easy low carb skillet bread with a wonderful crust of cheddar cheese. This keto bread recipe is perfect with soups and stews, and makes the BEST low carb Thanksgiving stuffing!

Prep Time 10 mins
Cook Time 16 mins
Total Time 26 mins
Servings: 10

Ingredients

- 1 tbsp butter for the skillet
- 2 cups almond flour
- 1/2 cup flax seed meal
- 2 tsp baking powder
- 1/2 tsp salt
- 1 & 1/2 cups shredded Cheddar cheese divided
- 3 large eggs lightly beaen
- 1/2 cup butter melted
- 3/4 cup almond milk

Instructions

- Preheat oven to 425F. Add 1 tbsp butter to a 10-inch oven-proof skillet and place in oven.
- In a large bowl, whisk together almond flour, flax seed meal, baking powder, salt and 1 cup of the shredded cheddar cheese.
- Stir in the eggs, melted butter and almond milk until thoroughly combined.
- Remove hot skillet from oven (remember to put on your oven mitts), and swirl butter to coat sides.
- Pour batter into pan and smooth the top. Sprinkle with remaining 1/2 cup cheddar.

- Bake 16 to 20 minutes, or until browned around the edges and set through the middle. Cheese on top should be nicely browned.
- Remove and let cool 15 minutes.

Recipe Notes

Serves 10. Each serving has 7.2 g of carbs and 4 g of fiber. Total NET CARBS = 3.2 g.

PALEO CHOCOLATE ZUCCHINI BREAD

Paleo Chocolate Zucchini Bread. Easy, Healthy Gluten free loaf, super moist with almond meal and unsweetened cocoa powder. 100% KETO + Low carb + sugar free

Prep Time10 mins
Cook Time50 mins
Cool down4 hrs
Total Time1 hr
Servings: 12 slices
Calories: 185kcal

Ingredients

Dry ingredients

- 1 1/2 cup almond flour (170g)
- 1/4 cup unsweetened cocoa powder (25g)
- 1 1/2 teaspoon baking soda
- 2 teaspoons ground cinnamon
- 1/4 teaspoon sea salt
- 1/2 cup sugar free crystal sweetener (Monk fruit or erythritol) (100g) or coconut sugar if refined sugar free

Wet ingredients

- 1 cup zucchini, finely grated measure packed, discard juice/liquid if there is some - about 2 small zucchini
- 1 large egg
- 1/4 cup + 2 tablespoon canned coconut cream 100ml
- 1/4 cup extra virgin coconut oil , melted, 60ml
- 1 teaspoon vanilla extract
- 1 teaspoon apple cider vinegar

Filling - optional

- 1/2 cup sugar free chocolate chips

- ❖ 1/2 cup chopped walnuts or nuts you like

Instructions

- ➢ Preheat oven to 180C (375F). Line a baking loaf pan (9 inches x 5 inches) with parchment paper. Set aside.
- ➢ Remove both extremity of the zucchinis, keep skin on.
- ➢ Finely grate the zucchini using a vegetable grater. Measure the amount needed in a measurement cup. Make sure you press/pack them firmly for a precise measure and to squeeze out any liquid from the grated zucchini, I usually don't have any!. If you do, discard the liquid or keep for another recipe.
- ➢ In a large mixing bowl, stir all the dry ingredients together: almond flour, unsweetened cocoa powder, sugar free crystal sweetener, cinnamon, sea salt and baking soda. Set aside.
- ➢ Add all the wet ingredients into the dry ingredients : grated zucchini, coconut oil, coconut cream, vanilla, egg, apple cider vinegar.
- ➢ Stir to combine all the ingredients together.
- ➢ Stir in the chopped nuts and sugar free chocolate chips.
- ➢ Transfer the chocolate bread batter into the prepared loaf pan.

- Bake 50 - 55 minutes, you may want to cover the bread loaf with a piece of foil after 40 minute to avoid the top to darken too much, up to you.
- The bread will stay slightly moist in the middle and firm up after fully cool down.

Cool down

- Cool down 10 minutes in the loaf pan, then cool down on a cooling rack until it reach room temperature. It can take 4 hours as it is a thick bread. Don' slice the bread before it reach room temperature. If too hot in the center, it will be too oft and fall apart when you slice. For a faster result, cool down 40 minutes at room temperature then pop in the fridge for 1 hour. The fridge will create an extra fudgy texture and the bread will be even easier to slice as it firms up.
- Store in the fridge up to 4 days in a cake bow or airtight container.

Nutrition Info

Calories: 185kcal

Carbohydrates: 6.1g

Protein: 4.9g

Fat: 17.1g

Fiber: 2.7g

Sugar: 1.2g

KETO FIBER BREAD ROLLS RECIPE

Perfectly made those Low Carb and Keto Fiber Bread Rolls Recipe are extremely delicious and irresistible to make. One look at them will convince you to try and make them right this moment.

Prep Time 10 minutes
Cook Time 40 minutes
Total Time 50 minutes

Serving: 11 Serving Size: 1

Ingredients

- 150g (1.5 Cups) Almond Flour
- 30g (1/4 Cup) Protein
- 1 Pkt (16g)(4tsp) Baking Powder
- 75g (3/4 Cup) Potato or Oat Fiber
- 15g (3Tbsp) Psyllium Husk
- 250g (1 Cup) Greek Yogurt
- 4 Eggs
- 4 Tbsp (25g) Oil
- 2 Tbsp Water
- 2 Tbsp Vinegar
- 1 tsp salt

Instructions

- Heat up the oven to 150C or 300F
- Mix all of the dry ingredience
- Separate eggs and mix all of the eggwhites first. Set aside
- Mix egg yolks fully.
- Add Yogurt and all of the wet ingredients

- Spoon by spoon keep adding all of the mixed dry ingredients
- At the end add egg whites and mix it gently and fully
- Cover the bowl and let it rest for half hour
- Prepare a baking sheet with Parchment paper
- Once rested, with wet hand make small balls, which you then flatten a bit at the end with hands to achieve rolls
- Once all is on the baking sheet, add a little bit of Potato or Oat Fiber to achieve the white look after baking
- With knife of your super Kaiser Roll Shaper Gadget press on each Roll to give it the perfect end touch
- Place it into the oven and bake for 40 Minutes
- Bon Appetit

Notes

For this recipe you can use Potato Fiber or Oat Fiber to achieve the results, which are identical.

Nutrition Info

Calories: 177
Total Fat: 14g
Carbohydrates: 7g
Fiber: 7g
Protein: 11g

3 INGREDIENT PALEO NAAN

Prep Time: 5 minutes Serving: 6 small naans Method: Stovetop Cuisine: Indian

Ingredients

- ❖ ½ cup almond flour
- ❖ ½ cup tapioca flour or arrowroot flour

- ❖ 1 cup coconut milk, canned and full fat
- ❖ Salt, adjust to taste, optional
- ❖ Ghee (slather that bread!), optional

Instructions

- ➢ Preheat a crepe pan OR nonstick pan over medium heat.
- ➢ Mix all the ingredients together in a bowl, and pour ¼ cup of the batter onto the pan.
- ➢ After the batter fluffs up and looks firm/mostly cooked, flip it over to cook the other side (be patient, this takes a little time!).
- ➢ Serve immediately or cool on a wire rack.

Notes

Options for Size:

- ➢ Have questions about this recipe? Check out my Paleo Naan FAQ
- ➢ If your naan is a bit sticky in the middle, you can put it on a baking sheet and bake for 5 minutes at 350F or for 10-15 minutes at 400F for a crispier flatbread.
- ➢ If you want to make a dessert crepe, pour the batter and spread it out as thin as you can.

- ➢ If you are not using a non-stick pan, you will need to use some sort of oil/ghee/fat to keep the batter from sticking. I have and love this carbon steel crepe pan.
- ➢ If the cream has solidified in your canned coconut milk, then mix well before using.

Nutrition Info

Calories Per Serving: 129

15% Total Fat 9.6g

0% Cholesterol 0mg

0% Sodium 6mg

4% Total Carbohydrate 11g

Sugars 1.4g

2% Protein 1g

KETO FATHEAD BAGELS

Truly chewy keto bagels - you want them and I've got them! These bagels are low carb, nut-free, and take only 5 ingredients to make. Easy and delicious, they will take your healthy breakfast to a whole new level.

Prep Time 20 mins
Cook Time 20 mins

Total Time 40 mins

Servings: 8 servings

Ingredients

- 1/2 cup coconut flour (56g)
- 2 tsp baking powder
- 3/4 tsp xanthan gum
- 12 oz pre-shredded part skim mozzarella
- 2 large eggs

Optional Topping for Everything Bagels

- 1 tsp sesame seeds
- 1 tsp poppyseed
- 1 tsp dried minced onion
- 1/2 tsp coarse salt
- 1 tbsp butter melted

Instructions

> Preheat the oven to 350F and line a large baking sheet with a silicone liner. In a medium bowl, whisk together the coconut flour, baking powder, and xanthan gum. Set aside.

- In a large microwave safe bowl, melt the cheese on high in 30 second increments until well melted and almost liquid. Stir in the flour mixture and the eggs and knead in the bowl using a rubber spatula.
- Turn out onto the prepared baking sheet and continue to knead together until cohesive. Cut the dough in half and cut each half into 4 equal portions so that you have 8 equal pieces of dough.
- Roll each portion out into a log about 8 inches long. Pinch the ends of the log together.
- In a shallow dish, stir together the sesame seeds, poppyseed, dried onion, and salt. Brush the top of each bagel with melted butter and dip firmly into the everything seasoning. Set back on the silicone mat.
- Bake 15 to 20 minutes, until the bagels have risen and are golden brown.

Nutrition Info

Calories 190 Calories from Fat 111

Total Fat 12.3g 19%

Total Carbohydrates 5.5g 2%

Dietary Fiber 2.6g 10%

Protein 12.1g 24%

CHEESY KETO GARLIC BREAD - USING MOZZARELLA DOUGH

The BEST recipe for cheesy keto garlic bread - using mozzarella dough. At only 1.5g net carbs per slice, this is an absolute keeper for your low-carb recipe folder.

Prep Time 10 mins
Cook Time 15 mins
Total Time 25 mins
Servings: 10

Ingredients

- 170 g pre shredded/grated cheese mozzarella
- 85 g almond meal/flour
- 2 tbsp cream cheese full fat
- 1 tbsp garlic crushed
- 1 tbsp parsley fresh or dried
- 1 tsp baking powder
- pinch salt to taste
- 1 egg medium

Instructions

- Place all the ingredients apart from the egg, in a microwaveable bowl. Stir gently to mix together. Microwave on HIGH for 1 minute.
- Stir then microwave on HIGH for a further 30 seconds.
- Add the egg then mix gently to make a cheesy dough.
- Place on a baking tray and form into a garlic bread shape. Cut slices into the low-carb garlic bread.
- Optional: Mix 2 tbsp melted butter, 1 tsp parsley and 1 tsp garlic. Brush over the top of the low-carb garlic bread, sprinkle with more cheese.
- Bake at 220C/425F for 15 minutes, or until golden brown.

Nutrition Info

Calories 117.4 Calories from Fat 88

Total Fat 9.8g 15%

Total Carbohydrates 2.4g 1%

Dietary Fiber 0.9g 4%

Sugars 0.6g

Protein 6.2g 12%

LOW CARB ASPARAGUS EGG BITES

These Asparagus Egg Bites make the perfect snack - especially on the go! Low carb, keto, and gluten free recipe.

Prep Time: 5 minutes
Cook Time: 15 minutes
Total Time: 20 minutes
Servings: 3

Ingredients

- ❖ non-stick cooking spray
- ❖ 3 medium asparagus stalks
- ❖ 6 eggs

- ❖ 1 tbs unsweetened almond milk
- ❖ salt and pepper
- ❖ 2 tbs grated Parmesan

Instructions

- ➢ Preheat the oven to 400F (200C).
- ➢ Prepare a six-hole muffin pan by spraying it liberally with some non-stick cooking spray. Chop up the asparagus (to make about half a cup) and divide between the muffin pan cups.
- ➢ Beat the eggs and unsweetened almond milk together in a jug. Season with salt and pepper then divide it between the muffin cups.
- ➢ Sprinkle some grated Parmesan over the top of each one, then bake in a preheated oven for 12-15 minutes, until golden brown on top and the egg is cooked through. They will puff up while cooking but deflate slightly as they cool.
- ➢ Remove the asparagus egg bites from the pan and enjoy warm - or let cool fully and store in the fridge.

Nutrition Info

Calories 143 Calories from Fat 81

Total Fat 9g 14%

Saturated Fat 3g 15%

Trans Fat 0g

Sodium 178mg 7%

Potassium 153mg 4%

Total Carbohydrates 1g 0%

Dietary Fiber 0g 0%

Sugars 0g

Protein 12g 24%

KETO CREAM CHEESE BREAD

Keto cream cheese bread is a low carb bread recipe that is made with coconut flour making it keto-friendly as well as nut-free.

Prep Time: 5 minutes
Cook Time: 25 minutes
Additional Time: 5 minutes
Total Time: 35 minutes
Serving: 12

Ingredients

- 8 large eggs
- 8 ounces of full-fat cream cheese (room temperature)
- ½ cup of unsalted butter (room temperature)
- 1 ½ cups coconut flour
- ½ cup of full-fat sour cream
- 4 teaspoons of baking powder
- 1 teaspoon of sea salt
- 1 tablespoon of sugar substitute
- 2 tablespoons of sesame seeds (optional)

Instructions

- Allow your eggs, cream cheese, butter to come to room temperature.
- Pre-heat your oven to 350 degrees.
- Grease a 12 cavity muffin pan generously with butter or a 10 inch loaf pan.
- In a medium-sized bowl combine your coconut flour, baking powder, sea salt, sugar substitute and set aside.
- In a large bowl using a handheld electric mixer or a standup mixer beat together the room temperature butter, cream cheese until light and fluffy. Be sure to

scrape the sides of bowl several times to make sure the mixture is well blended.

- To this butter and cream cheese mixture add the 8 eggs one at a time. Making sure to scrape the sides of the bowl several times. Note that due to the large number of eggs the mixture will not fully combine, this is normal. Once you add the dry ingredients to this wet mixture, the ingredients will come together perfectly.
- To the wet ingredients slowly add all the dry ingredients on a low mixing setting. Making sure to scrape the bowl a couple of times.
- Once the two mixtures are fully combined stop using the electric mixture and fold in the 1/2 cup of sour cream gently. Making sure the sour cream gets fully incorporated into the batter but being careful to not over mix. Note that the batter will be very thick and fluffy. This is the normal texture when using coconut flour exclusively in a recipe.
- Overfill the muffin pan just slightly. The thick batter will not cause the muffins to spread. Slightly overfilling your muffin tins will create a nice muffin top.
- With one additional whole egg and a tablespoon of water create an egg wash. Baste the top of each muffin with the egg wash and then sprinkle the sesame seeds on top of each muffin. This step is optional.

- Bake the muffins for 25-30 minutes until lightly brown on the top and when an inserted toothpick comes out clean.
- If you are baking your keto cream cheese bread in a 10 inch loaf, bake the bread for up to 90 minutes. Check your bread at 60 minutes for doneness and allow to cook longer if necessary.

Nutrition Info

Calories: 204

Total Fat: 19.4g

Saturated Fat: 11.4g

Cholesterol: 154mg

Sodium: 160mg

Carbohydrates: 2.2g

Fiber: 0.6g

Sugar: 0.4g

Protein: 5.8g

CHEDDAR GARLIC FATHEAD ROLLS

These keto dinner rolls are melt-in-your-mouth delicious. Made with cheddar cheese fathead dough, they are the perfect low carb side dish for all of your favorite meals. They make great sandwiches too.

Prep Time 10 mins
Cook Time 25 mins
Total Time 35 mins

Servings: 8 servings

Ingredients

Rolls:

- 8 ounces cheddar cheese grated (I used Cabot Vermont Cheddar)
- 2 tbsp butter
- 1/2 cup coconut flour
- 1/4 cup unflavored whey protein powder or egg white protein powder
- 4 tsp baking powder
- 1 tsp garlic powder
- 1/4 tsp salt
- 2 large eggs
- 1 large egg white

Garlic Butter

- 2 tbsp butter melted
- 2 cloves garlic minced
- 1 tbsp chopped parsley
- 1/2 tsp coarse salt

Instructions

- Preheat the oven to 350F and line an 8-inch round baking pan with parchment paper.
- In a large microwave safe bowl, combine the grated cheese and the butter. Melt on high in 30 second increments until the cheese and butter can be stirred together and is almost liquid.
- Add the coconut flour, protein powder, baking powder, garlic powder, and salt. Stir in the eggs and egg white and use a rubber spatula to "knead" together in the bowl until uniform.
- Divide the dough into 8 equal portions. The dough will be quite sticky so lightly oil your hands and roll into 8 ball. Place in the prepared baking pan.
- Whisk together the ingredients for the garlic butter and brush about half of it over the rolls in the pan.
- Bake 20 to 25 minutes, until puffed, golden brown, and firm to the touch. Remove and let cool about15 minutes before removing from the pan and breaking apart. Brush with the remaining garlic butter. Serve warm.

Nutrition Info

Calories 230 Calories from Fat 143

Total Fat 15.9g 24%

Total Carbohydrates 5.9g 2%

Dietary Fiber 2.6g 10%

Protein 12.2g 24%

HEALTHY 3 INGREDIENT MINI PALEO PIZZA BASES CRUSTS

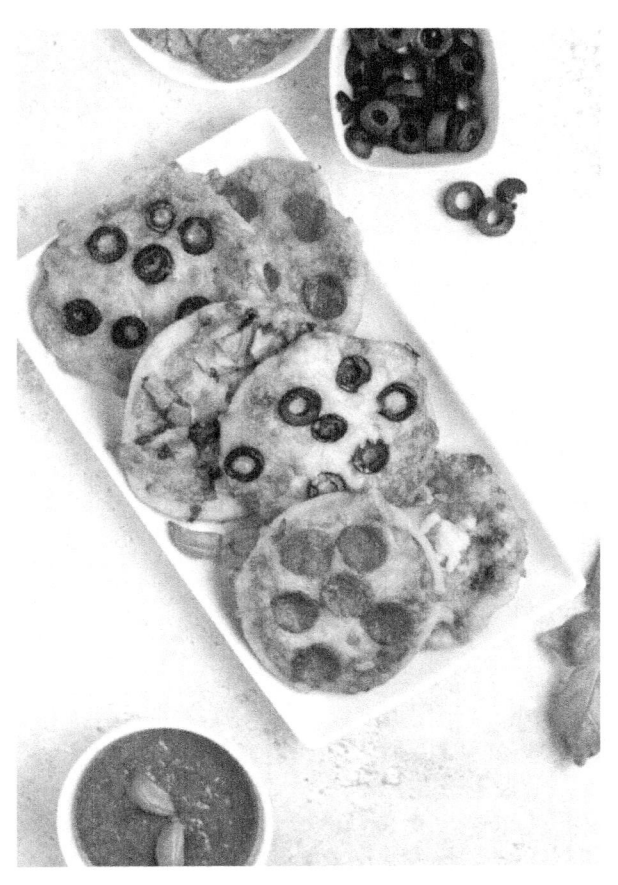

These 3 Ingredient mini paleo pizza crusts or bases are an easy, delicious and low carb alternative to traditional pizzas! Made with just three ingredients and on the stovetop, these 3 Ingredient Pizza bases are naturally gluten free, grain free, high protein, low calorie and have a nut free option!

Servings: 4

Calories: 125kcal

Ingredients

For the coconut flour option

- ❖ 8 large egg whites for thicker bases, use 5 whole eggs and 3 egg whites
- ❖ 1/4 cup coconut flour sifted
- ❖ 1/2 tsp baking powder
- ❖ Spices of choice salt, pepper, Italian spices
- ❖ Extra coconut flour to dust very lightly

For the almond flour option

- ❖ 8 large egg whites
- ❖ 1/2 cup almond flour
- ❖ 1/2 tsp baking powder
- ❖ Spices of choice salt, pepper, Italian spices

For the pizza sauce

- ❖ 1/2 cup Mutti tomato sauce
- ❖ 2 cloves garlic crushed
- ❖ 1/4 tsp sea salt

- ❖ 1 tsp dried basil

Instructions

To make the pizza bases/crusts

- ➤ In a large mixing bowl, whisk the eggs/egg whites until opaque. Sift in the coconut flour or almond flour and whisk very well until clumps are removed. Add the baking powder, mixed spices and continue to whisk until completely combined.
- ➤ On low heat, heat up a small pan and grease lightly.
- ➤ Once frying pan is hot, pour the batter in the pan and ensure it is fully coated. Cover the pan with a lid/tray for 3-4 minutes or until bubbles start to appear on top. Flip, cook for an extra 2 minutes and remove from pan- Keep an eye on this, as it can burn out pretty quickly.
- ➤ Continue until all the batter is used up.
- ➤ Allow pizza bases to cool. Once cool, use a skewer and poke holes roughly over the top, for even cooking. Dust very lightly with a dash of coconut flour.

To make the sauce

➢ Combine all the ingredients together and let sit at room temperature for at least 30 minutes- This thickens up.

Notes

- For a crispy pizza base, bake in the oven for 3-4 minutes prior to adding your toppings. If you want to freeze them, allow pizza bases to cool completely before topping with a dash of coconut flour and a thin layer of pizza sauce. Ensure each pizza base is divided with parchment paper before placing in the freezer.

Nutrition Info

Calories: 125kcal
Carbohydrates: 6g
Protein: 8g
Fat: 1g
Fiber: 3g

LOW CARB BLUEBERRY ENGLISH MUFFIN BREAD LOAF

Prep Time 15 minutes

Cook Time 45 minutes

Total Time 1 hour

Servings 12

Ingredients

- ❖ 1/2 cup almond butter or cashew or peanut butter
- ❖ 1/4 cup butter ghee or coconut oil
- ❖ 1/2 cup almond flour
- ❖ 1/2 tsp salt
- ❖ 2 tsp baking powder

- ❖ 1/2 cup almond milk unsweetened
- ❖ 5 eggs beaten
- ❖ 1/2 cup blueberries

Instructions

- ➢ Preheat oven to 350 degrees F.
- ➢ In a microwavable bowl melt nut butter and butter together for 30 seconds, stir until combined well.
- ➢ In a large bowl, whisk almond flour, salt and baking powder together. Pour the nut butter mixture into the large bowl and stir to combine.
- ➢ Whisk the almond milk and eggs together then pour into the bowl and stir well.
- ➢ Drop in fresh blueberries or break apart frozen blueberries and gently stir into the batter.
- ➢ Line a loaf pan with parchment paper and lightly grease the parchment paper as well.
- ➢ Pour the batter into the loaf pan and bake 45 minutes or until a toothpick in center comes out clean.
- ➢ Cool for about 30 minutes then remove from pan.
- ➢ Slice and toast each slice before serving.

Recipe Notes
Net Carbs: 3g

PARMESAN & TOMATO KETO BREAD BUNS

Prep Time: 10-15 minutes
Total Time: 55-60 minutes

Ingredients (makes 5 buns)

Dry ingredients:

- ❖ 3/4 cup almond flour (75 g/ 2.7 oz)

- 2 1/2 tbsp psyllium husk powder (20 g/ 0.7 oz)
- 1/4 cup coconut flour (30 g/ 1.1 oz)
- 1/4 cup packed cup flax meal (38 g/ 1.3 oz)
- 1 tsp cream of tartar or apple cider vinegar
- 1/2 tsp baking soda
- 2/3 cup grated Parmesan cheese (60 g/ 2.1 oz)
- 1/3 cup chopped sun-dried tomatoes (37 g/ 1.3 oz)
- 1/4 - 1/2 tsp pink sea salt
- 2 tbsp sesame seeds (18 g/ 0.6 oz) - or use 2 tbsp sunflower, flax, poppy seeds, or 1 tbsp caraway seeds

Wet ingredients:

- 3 large egg whites
- 1 large egg
- 1 cups boiling water (240 ml/ 8 fl oz)

Instructions

- Preheat the oven to 175 °C/ 350 °F (fan assisted). Use a kitchen scale to measure all the ingredients and add them to a mixing bowl (apart from the sesame seeds which are used for topping): almond flour, coconut flour, flax meal, psyllium husk powder, cream of tartar, baking soda, salt, parmesan cheese and sun dried

tomatoes. Mix all the dry ingredients together. Parmesan & Tomato Keto Bread Buns
- ➢ Add the egg whites and eggs and process well using a mixer until the dough is thick.
- ➢ The reason you shouldn't use only whole eggs is that the buns wouldn't rise with so many egg yolks in. Don't waste them - use them for making Home-made Mayo, Easy Hollandaise Sauce or Lemon Curd. Parmesan & Tomato Keto Bread Buns
- ➢ Add boiling water and process until well combined. Parmesan & Tomato Keto Bread Buns
- ➢ Using a spoon, divide the keto buns mix into 5 and roll into buns using your hands. Place them on a non-stick baking tray or on parchment paper. They will grow in size, so make sure to leave some space between them. You can even use small tart trays.
- ➢ Top each of the buns with sesame seeds (or any other seeds) and gently press them into the dough, so they don't fall out. Place in the oven and cook for about 45 - 50 minutes until golden on top. Parmesan & Tomato Keto Bread Buns
- ➢ Remove from the oven, let the tray cool down and place the buns on a rack to cool to room temperature. Parmesan & Tomato Keto Bread Buns

> Enjoy just like you would regular bread — with butter, ham or cheese! Parmesan & Tomato Keto Bread Buns Store in a tupperware for 2-3 days or freeze for up to 3 months.

Note: You Can make 5 regular/large buns as per recipe, or up to 10 small buns.

Nutrition Info

Calories 261 kcal
Net carbs 4.9 grams
Protein 14.5 grams
Fat 18.9 grams

GLUTEN FREE, PALEO & KETO DROP BISCUITS

Ultra tasty, easy, tender and moist. These gluten free, paleo and keto drop biscuits check all the right boxes! Whip them up in 30, for an awesome low carb bread that goes great with sweet and savory alike.

Prep Time: 10 minutes
Cook Time: 20 minutes
Total Time: 30 minutes
Servings: biscuits

Ingredients

- 1 egg
- 77 g sour cream or coconut cream + 2 tsp. apple cider vinegar, at room temp
- 2 tablespoons water
- 1 tablespoon apple cider vinegar
- 96 g almond flour
- 63 g golden flaxseed meal or psyllium husk, finely ground
- 21 g coconut flour
- 20 g whey protein isolate or more almond flour
- 3 1/2 teaspoons baking powder
- 1 teaspoon xanthan gum or 1 TBS. flaxseed meal
- 1/2 teaspoon kosher salt
- 112 g organic grass-fed butter or 7 TBS. ghee/coconut oil

Instructions

- Preheat oven to 450°F/230°C. Line a baking tray with parchment paper or a baking mat.

- Add eggs, sour (or coconut) cream, water and apple cider vinegar to a medium bowl and whisk for a minute or two until fully mixed. Set aside.
- Add almond flour, flaxseed meal, coconut flour, whey protein, baking powder, xanthan gum (or more flax) and kosher salt to a food processor and pulse until very thoroughly combined.
- Add in the butter and pulse a few times until pea-sized. Pour in the egg and cream mixture, pulsing until combined. The dough will be very shaggy.
- Drop 6 rounds of dough onto the prepared baking tray. Brush with melted butter and bake for 15-20 minutes until deep golden. Allow to cool for 10 minutes before serving. These guys keep well, stored in an airtight container at room temperature, for 3-4 days.
- You can freeze the shaped biscuit dough for 1-2 months, and bake straight from the freezer as needed.

Nutrition Info

Calories 290 Calories from Fat 270

Total Fat 30g 46%

Saturated Fat 11g 55%

Cholesterol 74mg 25%

Sodium 455mg 19%

Potassium 113mg 3%

Total Carbohydrates 8g 3%

Dietary Fiber 5g 20%

Sugars 1g

Protein 7g 14%

BUTTERY LOW CARB FLATBREAD

The best thing since sliced bread. Mostly because it's gluten-free, fried, and slathered in butter.

Prep time 5 mins
Cook time 2 mins
Total time 7 mins

Serves: 4

Ingredients

- 1 cup Almond Flour
- 2 tbsp Coconut Flour
- 2 tsp Xanthan Gum
- ½ tsp Baking Powder
- ½ tsp Falk Salt + more to garnish
- 1 Whole Egg + 1 Egg White
- 1 tbsp Water
- 1 tbsp Oil for frying
- 1 tbsp melted Butter-for slathering

Instructions

- Whisk together the dry ingredients (flours, xanthan gum, baking powder, salt) until well combined.
- Add the egg and egg white and beat gently into the flour to incorporate. The dough will begin to form.
- Add the tablespoon of water and begin to work the dough to allow the flour and xanthan gum to absorb the moisture.
- Cut the dough in 4 equal parts and press each section out with cling wrap. Watch the video for instructions!

- Heat a large skillet over medium heat and add oil.
- Fry each flatbread for about 1 min on each side.
- Brush with butter (while hot) and garnish with salt and chopped parsley.

Nutrition Info

Serving size: 1 flatbread

Calories: 232

Fat: 19

Carbohydrates: 9

Fiber: 5

Protein: 9

LOW CARB PALEO TORTILLAS RECIPE

If you're looking for easy coconut flour recipes, try paleo low carb tortillas with coconut flour. Just 3 ingredients in these keto paleo coconut wraps!

Prep Time 5 minutes
Cook Time 10 minutes
Total Time 15 minutes
Servings 8" tortillas

Ingredients

- ❖ 1/2 cup Coconut flour
- ❖ 6 large Eggs (up to 7-8)
- ❖ 1 1/4 cup Unsweetened almond milk (up to 1 1/2 cup; can also use any milk of choice - use coconut milk beverage for nut-free)
- ❖ 3/4 tsp Sea salt (optional)
- ❖ 1 tbsp Gelatin powder (optional - for more pliable, sturdy tortillas)
- ❖ 1/2 tsp Cumin (optional)
- ❖ 1/2 tsp Paprika (optional)

Instructions

- ➢ In a large bowl, whisk all ingredients together until smooth. Let the batter sit for a minute or two to account for the natural thickening caused by coconut flour. The batter should be very runny right before cooking - it should pour easily (add more almond milk and eggs in *equal* proportions if needed to achieve this). If you are using the optional gelatin, add an extra 1/4 cup almond milk.
- ➢ Heat a small skillet (about 8 in (20 cm) diameter) over medium to medium-high heat and grease lightly (use oil

of choice or an oil mister). Pour 1/4 cup (60 mL) of batter onto the skillet and immediately, rapidly tilt in different directions to evenly distribute, like making crepes. Cook, covered with a lid, until the edges are golden and you see bubbles forming in the middle. The edges will curl inward when you lift the lid (about 1-2 minutes). Flip over, cover again, and cook until browned on the other side (1-2 more minutes). Repeat until the batter is used up.

Recipe Notes

- Exact amounts of eggs and milk needed can vary slightly based on your brand of coconut flour, how tightly it sits in the measuring cup, etc.
- Ingredient amounts were adjusted slightly in September 2017, based on repeated experiments and feedback.
- A variation with optional gelatin is an option for more pliable, sturdy tortillas. This requires an extra 1/4 cup almond milk.
- Serving size: 1 8-inch tortilla. Nutrition Info does not include optional ingredients.

Nutrition Info

Calories 55

Fat 3g

Protein 5g

Total Carbs 4g

Net Carbs 1g

Fiber 3g

Sugar 1g

3 MINUTE LOW CARB BISCUITS

Prep Time: 2 minutes

Cook Time: 3 minutes

Total Time: 5 minutes

Servings: 1 Servings

Ingredients

- 1 tbsp Butter
- 2 tbsp Coconut flour
- 1 large Egg
- 1 tbsp Heavy Whipping Cream
- 2 tbsp Water
- 1/4 cup Cheddar Cheese
- 1/8 tsp garlic powder

- 1/8 tsp Onion powder
- 1/8 tsp Dried Parsley
- 1/8 tsp Pink Himalayan Salt
- 1/8 tsp black pepper
- 1/4 tsp Baking powder

Instructions

- Melt butter in a coffee mug by microwaving for 20 seconds.
- Add coconut flour, baking powder, and seasonings. Mix to incorporate with a fork.
- Add egg, water, cheese and heavy whipping cream. Mix until combined.
- Microwave for 3 minutes. Immediately remove from mug and allow to cool for 2 minutes.
- Slice and enjoy.

Nutrition Info

Calories: 392kcal
Carbohydrates: 9g
Protein: 15g
Fat: 32g
Fiber: 5g

KETO BANANA BREAD

A delicious version of Keto Banana Bread. I may be a little controversial with this recipe but I am providing options to satisfy all keto needs.

Prep Time: 10 minutes
Cook Time: 1 hour
Total Time: 1 hour 5 minutes
Servings: 16 serves

Ingredients

- 80 g butter melted
- 25 g sugar free maple syrup
- 1 cup (150g) Sukrin Gold sweetener or Lakanto Gold sweetener
- 2 teaspoons ground cinnamon
- 1/2 teaspoon nutmeg fresh grated
- 1 teaspoon vanilla
- 100 g banana
- 60 g golden flax meal or golden flax seeds milled extra fine
- 20 g coconut flour
- 150 g almond meal
- 1 tablespoon baking powder I totally recommend Bobs Red Mill Baking Powder for best rise
- 10 g psyllium husk powder or chia flour
- 1 teaspoon xanthan gum
- 4 eggs
- 80 g Greek natural yogurt

OPTIONAL

- 2 teaspoons banana extract INSTEAD of banana

- ❖ 1 cup walnuts or brazil nuts chopped

Instructions

- ➢ Preheat oven 170?. Line a 22cm x 11cm loaf tine with baking paper.

CONVENTIONAL METHOD

- ➢ Over medium heat cook butter, maple syrup, sweetener, cinnamon and nutmeg until butter has melted.
- ➢ In a large mixing bowl mash bananas. Pour in melted butter mixture and combine well.
- ➢ Add remaining ingredients including nuts (if using) and fold until combined.
- ➢ Scoop batter into prepared loaf tin. Smooth over top of loaf with wet spatula.
- ➢ Bake 60 minutes or until a skewer comes out clean. Cool 5 minutes in pan before transferring to wire rack to cool completely.

THERMOMIX METHOD

- Add butter, maple syrup, sweetener, cinnamon and nutmeg and cook 5 minutes/100?/stir.
- Add banana and mix 10 seconds speed 4. Scrape sides of bowl
- Add remaining ingredients. Mix 30 seconds/speed 3. Fold though nuts (if using) Follow instructions from Step 4 above.

Nutrition Info

Calories: 141kcal

Carbohydrates: 6g

Protein: 4g

Fat: 11g

Saturated Fat: 3g

Cholesterol: 51mg

Sodium: 63mg

Potassium: 150mg

Fiber: 2g

Sugar: 1g

HOT HAM AND CHEESE ROLL-UPS WITH DIJON BUTTER GLAZE

Prep/Cook Time: 40 minutes

Ingredients

For the Hot Ham and Cheese Roll-Ups

- ❖ 1/4 cup almond flour (get it here)

- ❖ 3 tablespoons coconut flour (get it here)
- ❖ 1 teaspoon onion powder
- ❖ 1 teaspoon garlic powder
- ❖ 1 1/2 cup low-moisture, part skim mozzarella cheese, shredded
- ❖ 4 tablespoons salted butter
- ❖ 2 tablespoons cream cheese
- ❖ 1 large pastured egg
- ❖ 10 ounces sliced ham
- ❖ 1 1/2 cups sharp white cheddar cheese, shredded

For the Dijon Butter Glaze

- ❖ 2 tablespoons salted butter
- ❖ 1 tablespoon Dijon mustard
- ❖ 1 teaspoon Worcestershire sauce
- ❖ 1 teaspoon garlic powder
- ❖ 1/2 teaspoon dried Italian seasoning

Instructions

- ➢ Preheat oven to 375°F.
- ➢ In a small mixing bowl, combine almond flour, coconut flour, onion powder and garlic powder.

- In a separate mixing bowl, combine mozzarella cheese, butter, and cream cheese. Microwave for 1 minute and 30 seconds to soften. Mix together until everything is well combined. If if gets stringy or is not quite melted enough, put it back in for another 30 seconds.
- To the cheese mixture, add the dry ingredients and the egg. Mix until all ingredients are well incorporated. If you are having a hard time mixing it, put it back in the microwave for another 20-30 seconds.
- Once the ingredients are combined, spread the dough out on parchment paper or a silpat in a thin and even layer – about 9 1/2 by 13 1/2. If it starts to get sticky, wet your hands a little bit to prevent it from sticking to you.
- Once you have the dough in a nice, even rectangle, sprinkle the cheddar over top, covering all of the dough.
- Next, layer on the ham.
- Roll the dough up tightly lengthwise. This will produce smaller rolls, but you will get almost twice as many. Turn so that the seam is facing down
- Cut the ends off each side of the roll-up to even it out. Then cut it into 1 1/2 slices.
- Place your individual roll-ups in a baking dish.
- Bake for 20-25 minutes or until they are fluffy and golden brown.

- ➢ While they are baking, melt the butter and mix it with the Dijon, Worcestershire, garlic powder and Italian seasoning. Fork whisk until all ingredients are well incorporated.
- ➢ Take your rolls out of the oven, brush the glaze over top of them. Return them to the oven and bake for an additional 5 minutes.

Nutrition Info

Calories – 482

Fat – 41g

Protein – 25g.

Carbs – 6.8g

Fiber – 2.8g

Net Carbs – 4g

SUNFLOWER PUMPKIN SEED PSYLLIUM BREAD

A low carb gluten free pumpkin sunflower seed psyllium bread. It's packed with hearty seeds and fiber. Enjoy it as a snack or along with a meal.

Prep Time 5 minutes
Cook Time 1 hour 10 minutes
Total Time 1 hour 15 minutes
Servings 10 people

Ingredients

- 1/4 teaspoon salt
- 3 tablespoons coconut oil melted
- 1 1/4 cup egg whites (300g) I used pasteurized in a carton
- 1/2 cup almond milk
- 1/2 cup whole psyllium husks finely ground, 60g
- 1/4 cup chia seeds 40g
- 1/4 cup pumpkin seeds 40g
- 1/4 cup sunflower seeds 40g
- 2 tablespoons flaxseed meal (15g) or sesame seed flour
- 1 teaspoon baking powder

Instructions

- In large mixing bowl, stir together psyllium, chia, pumpkin seeds, sunflower seeds, flax, baking powder, and salt.
- Stir in coconut oil.
- Blend in egg whites and almond milk being careful not to over mix.
- When thickened, spread out into a greased or lined 8x4-inch loaf pan.

> Bake for about 70 minutes at 325°F or until internal temperature reaches about 215°F.

Nutrition Info

Calories 155 Calories from Fat 72

Total Fat 8g 12%

Saturated Fat 4g 20%

Cholesterol 0mg 0%

Sodium 126mg 5%

Potassium 153mg 4%

Total Carbohydrates 14g 5%

Dietary Fiber 11g 44%

Sugars 0g

Protein 5g 10%

ROSEMARY AND GARLIC COCONUT FLOUR BREAD

Prep Time: 10 minutes

Cook Time: 45 minutes

Total Time: 55 minutes

Servings: 10 Slices

Ingredients

- 1/2 cup Coconut flour
- 1 stick butter (8 tbsp)
- 6 large eggs
- 1 tsp Baking powder
- 2 tsp Dried Rosemary
- 1/2-1 tsp garlic powder
- 1/2 tsp Onion powder
- 1/4 tsp Pink Himalayan Salt

Instructions

- Combine dry ingredients (coconut flour, baking powder, onion, garlic, rosemary and salt) in a bowl and set aside.
- Add 6 eggs to a separate bowl and beat with a hand mixer until you get see bubbles at the top.
- Melt the stick of butter in the microwave and slowly add it to the eggs as you beat with the hand mixer.
- Once wet and dry ingredients are fully combined in separate bowls, slowly add the dry ingredients to the wet ingredients as you mix with the hand mixture.
- Grease an 8x4 loaf pan and pour the mixture into it evenly.

- ➢ Bake at 350 for 40-50 minutes (time will vary depending on your oven).
- ➢ Let it rest for 10 minutes before removing from the pan. Slice up and enjoy with butter or toasted!

Nutrition Info

Calories: 147kcal

Carbohydrates: 3.5g

Protein: 4.6g

Fat: 12.5g

Fiber: 2g

KETO PALEO LOW-CARB STUFFING

A paleo-friendly, low-carb, keto stuffing made with homemade coconut flour bread. Savory and delicious for everyone at the holiday dinner table.

Prep time: 20 mins
Cook time: 30 mins

Total time: 50 mins

Serves: 12

Ingredients

- ½ teaspoon dried ground sage
- ¼ teaspoon black pepper
- ¼ teaspoon Himalayan rock salt
- ¼ teaspoon ground ginger
- ¼ teaspoon ground cinnamon
- ¾ cup homemade beef broth
- ¼ cup stevia-sweetened ginger ale (soda), or additional beef broth
- 1 loaf low-carb coconut flour bread
- ¼ cup fresh parsley
- 2 tablespoons tallow, coconut oil or red palm oil
- ½ red onion (200 grams), diced
- 4 celery sticks (200 grams), diced
- 2 teaspoons dried thyme leaves
- 1 teaspoon dried rosemary

Instructions

- Roughly chop fresh-baked bread into 1 inch chunks (it doesn't have to be perfect). Place the pieces on a large baking sheet and place in the oven (do not turn it on!). Keep it there for 24-48 hours. If it's still moist, let it sit in a 170F oven for about 1 hour or so. The bread should be a bit more moist than croutons, but not soft. This step will help the bread retain its shape in the stuffing, so don't skip it! Alternatively, you can dehydrate in your dehydrator, 130F for 24 hours.

- Place the bread chunks in a large bowl, toss with fresh parsley and set aside.
- Preheat oven to 350F and lightly grease a 2.3 L/2.5 qt. casserole dish with a dab of tallow, coconut oil or red palm oil.
- Heat tallow in a large pan on medium-high heat. Add onion and cook until soft, about 5 minutes. Add celery, thyme, rosemary, sage, pepper, salt, ginger and cinnamon. Cook for another 3 minutes.
- Remove from heat and add vegetable mixture to bread and toss to combine being sure not to over mix.
- Now, combine the beef broth and stevia-sweetened soda in a small dish. Pour the mixture over top of the bread. Again, be sure not to over mix, just toss, then add to the prepared casserole dish.
- Cover and bake in preheated oven for 30 minutes.
- Remove from the oven and let sit with the cover on for 5 minutes.

Nutrition Info

Calories: 234

Calories from Fat: 158.4

Total Fat: 17.6 g

Saturated Fat: 12.2 g

Cholesterol: 55 mg

Sodium: 169 mg

Carbs: 11.1 g

Dietary Fiber: 5.7 g

Net Carbs: 5.4 g

Sugars: 3.1 g

Protein: 7.7 g

15-MINUTE GLUTEN FREE, LOW CARB & KETO TORTILLAS

These 15-minute gluten free and keto tortillas are super pliable, easy and make the best low carb Mexican tacos!

Prep Time: 10 minutes
Cook Time: 5 minutes
Total Time: 15 minutes

Servings: 4

Ingredients

- 96 g almond flour
- 24 g coconut flour
- 2 teaspoons xanthan gum
- 1 teaspoon baking powder
- 1/8-1/4 teaspoon kosher salt depending on whether sweet or savory
- 2 teaspoons apple cider vinegar
- 1 egg lightly beaten
- 3 teaspoons water

Instructions

- Add almond flour, coconut flour, xanthan gum, baking powder and salt to food processor. Pulse until thoroughly combined.
- Pour in apple cider vinegar with the food processor running. Once it has distributed evenly, pour in the egg. Followed by the water. Stop the food processor once the dough forms into a ball. The dough will be sticky to touch.

- Wrap dough in cling film and knead it through the plastic for a minute or two. Think of it a bit like a stress ball. Allow dough to rest for 10 minutes (and up to two days in the fridge).
- Heat up a skillet (preferably) or pan over medium heat. You can test the heat by sprinkling a few water droplets, if the drops evaporate immediately your pan is too hot. The droplets should 'run' through the skillet.
- Break the dough into eight 1" balls (26g each). Roll out between two sheets of parchment or waxed paper with a rolling pin or using a tortilla press (easier!) until each round is 5-inches in diameter.
- Transfer to skillet and cook over medium heat for just 3-6 seconds (very important). Flip it over immediately (using a thin spatula or knife), and continue to cook until just lightly golden on each side (though with the traditional charred marks), 30 to 40 seconds. The key is not to overcook them, as they will no longer be pliable or puff up.
- Keep them warm wrapped in kitchen cloth until serving. To rewarm, heat briefly on both sides, until just warm (less than a minute).
- These tortillas are best eaten straight away. But feel free to keep some dough handy in your fridge for up to three days.

Notes

- When cooking, coconut flour burns rather rapidly. So while this does help you to get the traditional charred marks of flour tortillas, you do need to keep an eye out for them to keep them from burning. Having said that, you do want your skillet to be very hot in order for the tortillas to cook quickly (in under a minute) and stay pliable. Like any tortilla, if the heat is not high enough it will harden and crack.

Nutrition Info

Calories 89 Calories from Fat 54

Total Fat 6g 9%

Saturated Fat 1g 5%

Cholesterol 20mg 7%

Sodium 51mg 2%

Potassium 58mg 2%

Total Carbohydrates 4g 1%

Dietary Fiber 2g 8%

Protein 3g 6%

COCONUT FLOUR MINI CHEESE LOAVES

The perfect little cheesy mini loaf for lunch boxes. Serve warm with butter.

Prep Time 10 mins
Cook Time 15 mins
Total Time 25 mins
Servings: 1

Ingredients

- 8 eggs - medium
- 0.5 spring onion finely sliced
- 100 g grated/shredded cheese
- Coconut Flour Mini Cheese Loaves Toppings
- 1 pepperoni stick sliced
- 2 tbsp pumpkin seeds
- 113 g butter softened
- 50 g coconut flour
- 1 tsp baking powder
- salt and pepper to taste
- pinch chilli optional

Instructions

- Mix the softened butter with the coconut flour, baking powder salt, pepper and chilli (optional) until smooth.
- Add the eggs one at a time. Stir after each egg is added.
- Gently stir through the sliced spring onion and grated/shredded cheese (reserve some to top each loaf).
- Fill each mini loaf tin (or muffin cases).

- ➢ I like to top my mini loaves with a few pepperoni stick slices, then cover with some grated/shredded cheese and finally sprinkle a few pumpkin seeds over.
- ➢ Bake at 180C/350F for 15 minutes, or until golden.

Nutrition Info

Calories 170 Calories from Fat 124

Total Fat 13.8g 21%

Saturated Fat 8g 40%

Total Carbohydrates 2.8g 1%

Dietary Fiber 1.5g 6%

Sugars 0.6g

Protein 6.4g 13

COCONUT FLOUR PSYLLIUM HUSK BREAD – PALEO

Want an easy low carb keto Paleo bread? Try this gluten free coconut flour psyllium bread recipe. It's a tasty bread to serve with breakfast or dinner.

Prep Time 5 minutes
Cook Time 55 minutes
Total Time 1 hour
Servings 15 slices
Calories 127kcal

Ingredients

- 6 tablespoons whole psyllium husks 27g, may want to finely grind
- 3/4 cup warm water
- 1 cup coconut flour 125g
- 1 1/2 teaspoons baking soda
- 3/4 teaspoon sea salt
- 1 pint egg whites 2 cups (or use 8 whole eggs)
- 2 large eggs
- 1/2 cup olive oil
- 1/4 cup coconut oil melted

Instructions

- Preheat oven to 350°F.
- If not using silicone pan, grease or line pan with parchment paper. I used an 8x4-in pan.
- Dump all ingredients into a food processor and pulse until well combined. If you don't have a food processor, you can use a mixing bowl with electric mixer.
- Spread batter into 8x4 loaf pan. Smooth top.
- Bake for 45-55 minutes or until edges are brown and toothpick inserted comes out clean.

➢ Let bread sit in pan for 15 minutes. Remove bread from pan and allow to cool completely on rack.

Notes

Original recipe used a carton of eggs which can result in an ammonia smell. Therefore, the recipe has changed to use 1 pint egg whites and 2 whole eggs.

Nutrition Info

Calories 127 Calories from Fat 120

Total Fat 13.3g 20%

Sodium 243mg 10%

Total Carbohydrates 6g 2%

Dietary Fiber 4.1g 16%

Protein 3g 6%

CAULIFLOWER TORTILLAS

Great low carb alternative to traditional corn or flour tortillas.

Prep Time 30 minutes
Cook Time 20 minutes
Total Time 50 minutes
Servings 6 tortillas

Ingredients

- ❖ 3/4 large head cauliflower (or two cups riced)
- ❖ 2 large eggs (Vegans, sub flax eggs)
- ❖ 1/4 cup chopped fresh cilantro

- ❖ 1/2 medium lime, juiced and zested
- ❖ salt & pepper, to taste

Instructions

- ➢ Preheat the oven to 375 degrees F., and line a baking sheet with parchment paper.
- ➢ Trim the cauliflower, cut it into small, uniform pieces, and pulse in a food processor in batches until you get a couscous-like consistency. The finely riced cauliflower should make about 2 cups packed.
- ➢ Place the cauliflower in a microwave-safe bowl and microwave for 2 minutes, then stir and microwave again for another 2 minutes. If you don't use a microwave, a steamer works just as well. Place the cauliflower in a fine cheesecloth or thin dishtowel and squeeze out as much liquid as possible, being careful not to burn yourself. Dishwashing gloves are suggested as it is very hot.
- ➢ In a medium bowl, whisk the eggs. Add in cauliflower, cilantro, lime, salt and pepper. Mix until well combined. Use your hands to shape 6 small "tortillas" on the parchment paper.
- ➢ Bake for 10 minutes, carefully flip each tortilla, and return to the oven for an additional 5 to 7 minutes, or

until completely set. Place tortillas on a wire rack to cool slightly.
- ➢ Heat a medium-sized skillet on medium. Place a baked tortilla in the pan, pressing down slightly, and brown for 1 to 2 minutes on each side. Repeat with remaining tortillas.

Nutrition Info

Calories 357

Calories from Fat 276

Total Fat 30.63g 47%

Total Carbohydrates 7.9g 3%

Dietary Fiber 4.77g 19%

Protein 12.48g 25%

ROSEMARY OLIVE BREAD

This rosemary olive bread is baked with coconut flour in the shape of a circular loaf. Although the shape is not mandatory, it looks pretty.

Prep Time: 10 minutes
Cook Time: 35 minutes
Total Time: 45 minutes
Servings: 10 Slices

Ingredients

- 1/2 cup Coconut flour
- 4 medium Eggs

- 4 tablespoons Olive oil
- 2 tablespoons Pysllium husk powder
- 1 tablespoon Apple cider vinegar
- 1 tablespoon Baking powder
- 1/2 teaspoon Salt
- 1 1/2 tablespoons Rosemary dried or fresh
- 75 grams Black or green olives chopped
- 1/2 cups Boiling water

Instructions

- Preheat the oven to 180C/350F degrees
- Place the coconut flour, baking powder, rosemary, psyllium husk powder and salt in a bowl and mix thoroughly.
- Add the oil and eggs and blend well until the mixture looks like breadcrumbs.
- Add the apple cider vinegar and mix well.
- Add the chopped olives to the bread and mix.
- Gently add the water, a bit at time and stir into the mixture (you may not need it all).
- Line a baking tray with parchment paper.
- Using your hands, make a large ball of the dough (I find keeping my hands wet helps with the sticky dough).

- Place the dough on the parchment paper lined baking tray.
- Score the top to make a pattern is optional!
- Bake for 35 minutes until golden and firm.
- Eat and enjoy!

Nutrition Info

Serving: 1 Slice

Calories: 123kcal

Carbohydrates: 6g

Protein: 3g

Fat: 9g

WHOLEMEAL SEED & GRAIN APRICOT LOAF BY ALLINSON'S

Total Time 3h 5m

Prep Time 2h 30m

Bake Time 35m

Serves 8

Ingredients

- 500g Allinson's Wholemeal Seed & Grain Bread Flour
- 1 tsp Salt

- 1 tsp Silver Spoon Caster Sugar
- 7g Allinson's Easy Bake Yeast

- Perfect to use in bread makers and hand baking this yeast, gives your dough a quick rise, eliminating the need to 'knock back.' The dough will only require one kneading and one period of proving. The yeast can be added with the flour straight from the pack and will become activated as soon as it comes into contact with the liquid.
- 75g Dried Apricots (Chopped)
- 2 tbsp Extra Virgin Olive Oil
- 300ml Tepid Water

Instructions

- Mix together the flour, salt and sugar in a large bowl. Stir in the yeast and apricots. Mix the oil and water together.

- Make a well in the centre of the flour mixture and add the warm water and oil mix. Mix together until a soft dough starts to form. Turn the dough onto a lightly floured surface. Knead until smooth and elastic, this can

- take up to 10 minutes. This could also be done using a dough hook of your free-standing mixer.
- Lightly grease a clean mixing bowl. Cover the bowl with oiled cling film or a damp tea cloth and leave to rise in a warm place for about 45 minutes - 1 hour or until the dough has doubled in size.
- Knock back the dough by gently kneading just 5 times to get the air out. Mould into a smooth oval and lift into a lightly oiled 900g (23 x 13cm) loaf tin.
- Cover the dough with oiled cling film or a damp tea cloth and leave to rise in a warm place for about 45 minutes - 1 hour or until the dough has doubled in size.
- Preheat your oven to 200°C, fan 180°C, gas mark 6.
- Slit the dough in a criss cross pattern with a sharp knife and sprinkle the dough with a little flour to create a crisp, rustic coating on top of the bread. Bake for 30 - 35 minutes or until the bread is risen, golden brown and sounds hollow when tapped underneath.
- Turn the bread out onto a wire rack as soon as possible to avoid a soggy crust on the bottom.

Let's Bake

KETO CHEDDAR JALAPEÑO "CORNBREAD"

Light and fluffy Low Carb and Keto friendly version of cornbread with cheddar cheese and fresh chopped jalapeño peppers!

Prep Time 5 mins
Cook Time 40 mins
Total Time 45 mins

Ingredients

- ❖ 2 Cups Almond Flour
- ❖ 2 tablespoons Oat Fiber ,
- ❖ 3 Eggs, beaten
- ❖ 1 Cup Sour Cream
- ❖ ½ cup baby corn, chopped
- ❖ ¼ cup fresh jalapeño peppers, chopped
- ❖ ½ cup Grass-Fed Butter, melted
- ❖ 1 Cup Shredded Cheddar Cheese
- ❖ 3 teaspoons swerve confectioners, or powdered erythritol
- ❖ 1 tablespoon Baking Powder
- ❖ ½ teaspoon baking soda
- ❖ Pinch of Salt
- ❖ Optional: 1 jalapeño sliced into thin rings for topping

Instructions

- ➢ Preheat oven to 350F.
- ➢ Whisk all the dry ingredients together in a bowl and set aside. In a separate bowl, add the eggs, sour cream, swerve and butter, then mix to combine. Add in the jalapeño peppers, cheddar cheese and baby corn.

- ➢ Mix in the dry ingredients, just until combined. Pour the mixture into an 8 X 8 glass or ceramic baking dish that's been sprayed with nonstick spray.
- ➢ Optional: Top with the thinly sliced jalapeño pepper rings. Bake for 40-45 minutes or until a toothpick, when inserted, comes out clean. Store leftovers in the fridge for several days or freeze. It thaws and reheats perfectly!

Nutrition Info

Calories 271

Calories from Fat 225

Fat 25g

Saturated Fat 10g

Carbohydrates 6g

Fiber 3g13%

Sugar 2g2%

Protein 9g

ROSEMARY AND GARLIC COCONUT FLOUR BREAD

A nut-free low-carb bread made with coconut flour and flavored with herbs.

Total Time 55 minutes

Prep Time: 10 minutes
Cook Time: 45 minutes
Servings 10 Slices

Ingredients:

- 1/2 cup Coconut flour
- 1 stick butter (8 tbsp)
- 6 large eggs
- 1 tsp Baking powder
- 2 tsp Dried Rosemary
- 1/2-1 tsp garlic powder
- 1/2 tsp Onion powder
- 1/4 tsp Pink Himalayan Salt

Instructions:

- Combine dry ingredients (coconut flour, baking powder, onion, garlic, rosemary and salt) in a bowl and set aside.
- Add 6 eggs to a separate bowl and beat with a hand mixer until you get see bubbles at the top.
- Melt the stick of butter in the microwave and slowly add it to the eggs as you beat with the hand mixer.
- Once wet and dry ingredients are fully combined in separate bowls, slowly add the dry ingredients to the wet ingredients as you mix with the hand mixture.
- Grease an 8x4 loaf pan and pour the mixture into it evenly.

- Bake at 350 for 40-50 minutes (time will vary depending on your oven).
- Let it rest for 10 minutes before removing from the pan. Slice up and enjoy with butter or toasted!

Nutrition Info

Calories 147

Calories from Fat 113

Fat 12.5g

Carbohydrates 3.5g

Fiber 2g

Protein 4.6g

EASY KETO ZUCCHINI BREAD RECIPE WITH BACON AND CHEESE

Prep Time: 15 mins

Cook Time: 50 mins

Total Time: 1 hr 5 mins

Servings: 12 serves

Ingredients

- 3 ounces almond flour
- 2 ounces coconut flour
- 1/2 teaspoon salt
- 1/2 teaspoon pepper
- 2 teaspoons baking powder
- 1 teaspoon xanthan gum
- 5 large eggs
- 2/3 cup butter melted
- 4 ounces cheddar cheese grated
- 6 ounces zucchini grated and liquid squeezed out
- 6 ounces bacon diced

Instructions

- Preheat oven to 175C/350F.
- In a large bowl add the almond flour, coconut flour, salt, pepper, baking powder and xanthan gum. Mix well.
- Add the eggs and melted butter and mix well.
- Fold through ¾ of the cheddar, along with the zucchini and bacon.
- Spoon into your greased 9in ceramic loaf dish (if using a meat dish, line with parchment paper) and bake for 35

- minutes, remove from the oven and top with the remaining cheese.
- ➢ Bake for another 10-15 minutes, until the cheese has browned and a skewer comes out clean.
- ➢ Leave to cool for 20 minutes.
- ➢ Slice into 12 slices and enjoy warm.

Nutrition Info

Calories: 281kcal

Carbohydrates: 5g

Protein: 9g

Fat: 25g

Saturated Fat: 11g

Cholesterol: 123mg

Sodium: 387mg

Potassium: 173mg

Fiber: 3g

Sugar: 1g

KETO JALAPEÑO CHEESE BREAD

This keto jalapeño cheese bread is reminiscent of pizza bread! Only requiring one bowl this is an easy low-carb, nut-free bread option to whip up for sandwiches, a snack, or simply a side.

Ingredients (makes 8 servings)

- ❖ 4 large eggs
- ❖ 2 heaped tbsp full-fat Greek yogurt (60 g/ 2.1 oz)
- ❖ 1/3 cup coconut flour (40 g/ 1.4 oz)
- ❖ 2 tbsp whole psyllium husks (8 g/ 0.3 oz)
- ❖ 1/2 tsp sea salt

- ❖ 1 tsp gluten-free baking powder
- ❖ 1/2 cup shredded sharp cheddar cheese, divided (57 g/ 2 oz)
- ❖ 1/4 cup diced pickled jalapeños (28 g/ 1 oz)
- ❖ few sliced jalapeños for topping (14 g/ 0.5 oz)
- ❖ Optional: serve with homemade Marinara Sauce or Ranch Dressing

Instructions

- ➢ Preheat the oven to 190 °C/ 375 °F (conventional), or 170 °C/ 340 °F (fan assisted) and line a baking sheet with parchment paper. In a medium bowl whisk together the eggs and Greek yogurt. Keto Jalapeño Cheese Bread
- ➢ Add coconut flour, psyllium husks, salt and baking powder. Keto Jalapeño Cheese Bread
- ➢ Once smooth stir in half of the shredded cheddar cheese. Keto Jalapeño Cheese Bread
- ➢ Add the diced jalapeños. Keto Jalapeño Cheese Bread
- ➢ Press the dough into a 2.5 cm/ 1 inch thick sphere on the baking sheet. Top with remaining cheese and additional jalapeños if desired. Keto Jalapeño Cheese Bread

- Bake for 15 minutes or until golden and fluffy. Cut into 8 squares. Keto Jalapeño Cheese Bread
- Serve warm or let it cool down. Keto Jalapeño Cheese Bread Store in an airtight container in the refrigerator for up to 7 days.

Nutrition Info

Net carbs1.5 grams
Protein6.4 grams
Fat5.9 grams
Calories92 kcal

KETO CLOUD BREAD ("OOPSIE BREAD")

This low-carb cloud bread (also called "oopsie bread") has only four ingredients, is keto-friendly, and clocks in with less than half a gram of net carbs.

Prep Time: 10 minutes
Cook Time: 30 minutes
Total Time: 40 minutes
Servings: 10 pieces

Ingredients

- ❖ 3 eggs, room temperature
- ❖ 3 tbsp cream cheese, softened
- ❖ 1/4 tsp cream of tartar

- ❖ 1/4 tsp salt
- ❖ 1 scoop Perfect Keto Unflavored Whey Protein Powder (Optional)

Instructions

- ➢ Preheat oven to 300°F and line two baking sheets with parchment paper.
- ➢ Carefully separate egg whites from yolks. Place whites in one bowl and yolks in another.
- ➢ In the bowl of egg yolks, add cream cheese and mix together with a hand mixer until well-combined.
- ➢ In the bowl of egg whites, add cream of tartar and salt. Using a hand mixer, mix together at high speed until stiff peaks form.
- ➢ Pouring slowly, use a spatula or spoon to add yolk mixture to egg whites and carefully fold in until there are no white streaks.
- ➢ Spoon mixture onto prepared baking sheet about ½ to ¾ inches tall and about 5 inches apart.
- ➢ Bake in the oven on middle rack for 30 minutes, until tops are lightly golden brown.
- ➢ Allow to cool (they will likely be too crumbly directly out of the oven) and enjoy.

Nutrition Info

Serving Size: 1 piece

Calories: 35

Fat: 2.8g

Carbohydrates: 0.4g

Protein: 2.2g

EVERYTHING KETO ROLLS

Try your hand at these simple keto rolls. Cover them with everything spice, or whatever your heart desires. The rolls are simple to put together, and have NO egg taste to them at all!!

Cook Time 1 hour
Total Time 1 hour

Ingredients

- 120 grams of sunflower seed flour
- 5 tablespoons of ground psyllium husk
- 2 tsp baking powder
- 1/2 tsp salt
- 1 and 1/4th cup boiling water

- ❖ 2 tsp apple cider vinegar
- ❖ 1 tablespoon everything but the bagel seasoning + 1 tablespoon for the tops
- ❖ 3 Egg whites- I used organic ones from a carton so I don't have to find a use for the yokes. If you use whites from the carton its 6 tablespoons.
- ❖ Grated cheese for the tops is optional

Instructions

- ➢ Pre-heat oven to 350 and line a baking sheet with parchment
- ➢ Mix your sunflower seed flour, ground psyllium husk, baking powder, salt and seasoning in a bowl and whisk until combined
- ➢ Add the boiling water and mix for about a minute. You may need to switch to a spatula or wooden spoon instead of a whisk now.
- ➢ Add the apple cider vinegar and mix again.
- ➢ Finally when the mix has cooled a bit add the egg whites to the bowl. The mix will be well formed and it may seem that the eggs whites won't incorporate- just keep mixing and folding. Knead the dough with greased hands until everything is incorporated. It won't take long.

- With greased hands form 6 balls. The dough is fairly loose and slightly sticky but you can still make balls.
- Sprinkle your seasoning over the top and press it in so it sticks.
- Cook in the oven for 45 min- remove from oven and top with cheese if desired and then bake the remaining 15 minutes.
- Let fully cool before cutting open!
- Store in an airtight container in the fridge.

Nutrition Info

Calories: 155

Total Fat: 10g

Carbohydrates: 5g

Protein: 8g

KETO LOW CARB BANANA BREAD RECIPE WITH ALMOND FLOUR

This low carb banana bread recipe with almond flour & coconut flour is perfectly moist & rich. No one will know it's keto banana bread! Naturally paleo, gluten-free, sugar-free, and healthy.

Prep Time 10 minutes
Cook Time 1 hour

Total Time 1 hour 10 minutes

Ingredients

- 2 cupWholesome Yum Blanched Almond Flour
- 1/4 cupWholesome Yum Coconut Flour
- 1/2 cupWalnuts (chopped; plus more for topping if desired)
- 2 tspGluten-free baking powder
- 2 tspCinnamon
- 1/4 tspSea salt (optional)
- 6 tbspButter (softened; can use coconut oil for dairy-free, but flavor and texture will be different)
- 1/2 cupBesti Allulose *
- 1/2 tspXanthan gum (optional**, for more structure)
- 4 large Egg
- 1/4 cupUnsweetened almond milk
- 2 tspBanana extract

Instructions

- Preheat the oven to 350 degrees F. Line a 9x5 in (23x13 cm) loaf pan with parchment paper, so that the paper hangs over two opposite sides (for easy removal later).

- In a large bowl, mix together the almond flour, coconut flour, baking powder, cinnamon, and sea salt (if using).
- In another large bowl, use a hand mixer to butter and sweetener until fluffy. Beat in the eggs (use the low setting to avoid splashing). Stir in the banana extract and almond milk.
- Pour the dry ingredients into the wet. Beat on low setting until a dough/batter forms.
- Stir in the chopped walnuts.
- Transfer the batter into the lined loaf pan and press evenly to make a smooth top. If desired, sprinkle the top with additional chopped walnuts and press them lightly into the surface.
- Bake for 50-60 minutes, until an inserted toothpick comes out clean.
- Cool completely before removing from the pan and slicing. (The longer you let it sit before slicing, the better it will hold together. The next day is ideal if possible.)

Nutrition Info

Calories 224

Fat 20g

Protein 8g

Total Carbs 6g

Net Carbs 2g

Fiber 4g

Sugar 1g

KETO SPINACH DIP STUFFED BREAD

Prep Time: 20m
Cook Time: 25m
Total Time: 45m
Serves: 12

Ingredients

"Bread" Dough

- ❖ 5 ounces shredded mozzarella
- ❖ 1 ounce shredded cheddar
- ❖ 1 ounce cream cheese
- ❖ 1 tablespoon butter
- ❖ 1/2 teaspoon Italian seasoning

- 1/2 teaspoon garlic powder
- 1/2 cup + 2 tablespoons blanched almond flour
- 1 tablespoon oat fiber
- 1/2 teaspoon xantham gum
- 1 teaspoon baking powder
- 1 teaspoon active dry yeast
- 2 tablespoons warm (~110F) water, for dissolving yeast
- 2 large eggs (one for dough, one for egg wash)
- 1 tablespoon coconut (or almond) flour, for kneading dough

Filling

- 1 1/2 cups keto spinach dip
- 1 ounce shredded cheddar or mozzarella
- 2 tablespoons grated parmesan

Instructions

- Preheat oven to 375F. Prepare 9" round baking pan by thoroughly greasing, or a baking sheet by lining with parchment paper.
- Add yeast to warm water and allow to dissolve, stirring to break up any clumps.

- Sift together dry ingredients (almond flour, oat fiber, xantham gum, baking powder, garlic powder, Italian seasoning).
- In a microwave-safe bowl, combine shredded cheeses, cream cheese, and butter. Microwave for 60-90 seconds, or until cheese is melted. Stir to combine.
- Add dry ingredients, one egg, and yeast mixture to melted cheese mixture and mix well until dough forms a ball. Turn dough onto a flat surface sprinkled with the coconut flour and knead gently, 15-20 times or until no longer "sticky" to the touch.
- Optional: For best results, cover the dough with a damp cloth and allow to rise in a warm place for 10-15 minutes.
- Divide dough into two approximately equal sections, and roll each into a ~9" circle.
- Spread the spinach dip on one circle of dough, stopping just before the edges. Top with shredded cheese and parmesan. Layer the other circle of dough on top of the filling.
- Make 12 slices (like cutting a pizza) through both layers of dough, being careful to leave them connected in the center. Pick up each "slice" and twist gently so that the "bottom" layer of dough is on top.

- Beat the remaining egg and evenly brush the the exposed dough with the egg wash.
- Bake in the preheated oven for about 25 minutes, or until golden brown. Optionally, brush with melted garlic butter before serving.
- Best served warm. Store refrigerated for up to 5 days. Reheat in the microwave or in the oven at a low (~250F) temperature.

CHEESY KETO HAMBURGER BUNS

Total Time: 20 minutes

Servings: 6 buns

Ingredients

- ❖ 2 cups mozzarella cheese (shredded)
- ❖ 4 oz. cream cheese
- ❖ 4 large eggs
- ❖ 3 cups almond flour
- ❖ 4 tbsp. melted grass-fed butter

❖ Sesame seeds

Instructions

➢ Preheat oven to 400°F.
➢ Line a baking sheet with parchment paper.
➢ In a large bowl, combine mozzarella and cream cheese. Heat in the microwave for 10 seconds, or until both cheeses are melted.
➢ Add 3 eggs to your cheese mixture, and stir to combine. Add your almond flour, then stir again.
➢ Form dough into 6 bun-shaped balls then place on prepared baking sheet.
➢ Whisk your last egg. Brush each dough ball with melted butter and your whisked egg, then sprinkle with sesame seeds.
➢ Bake until golden, about 10-12 minutes.

Nutrition Info

Serving Size: 1 roll

Calories: 287

Fat: 25.8g

Carbohydrates: 2.4g

Protein: 14.7

ZUCCHINI COCONUT BREAD

Prep Time 10 minutes
Cook Time 45 minutes
Total Time 55 minutes
Servings 10

Ingredients

- 3/4 cup coconut flour
- 1/2 cup zucchini (grated and drained)
- 1/4 cup Pecan (chopped)
- 3/4 tbsp baking powder
- 1 tsp vanilla extract
- 1 scoop unflavored protein powder (around 28 - 30g)

- ❖ 6 large eggs
- ❖ 1/2 cup butter salted
- ❖ 1/2 cup So Nourished Erythritol (or less, up to your liking)
- ❖ 1/2 teaspoon salt

Instructions

- ➤ Preheat your oven to 350°F.
- ➤ Rinse the zucchini well with water and use a hand grater to shred it. Salt the grated zucchini in a bowl. Move to a colander to drain any unnecessary liquids. You should obtain about 1/2 cup of drained and shredded zucchini.
- ➤ Start making the dry mixture in a bowl. Fold the coconut flour, baking powder, and protein powder with the sweetener. Mix until blended entirely.
- ➤ Beat the eggs in a mixer together with vanilla extract and melted butter. Transfer the grated zucchini in and carefully add the dry mixture too. Whisk together until incorporated. Drop the chopped pecan.
- ➤ Coat a loaf pan with melted butter. Evenly spread the bread batter into the pan. Place in the oven for 40-45 minutes or until the bread is browned and cooked. Once

the surface turns golden, take out from the oven and let sit for 10 minutes before removing from the pan.
- ➢ Slice and enjoy!

Nutrition Info

Calories 177

Calories from Fat 135

Fat 15g

Saturated Fat 8g

Cholesterol 123mg

Sodium 255mg

Potassium 154mg

Carbohydrates 6g

Fiber 3g

Sugar 1g

Protein 5g

CONCLUSION

If you were to mention the word Ketogenic to the average fitness enthusiast, they might think you were talking about one of the characters from the latest Star Trek movie. While the name is not familiar, what Ketogenic's does is and you just may want to try it for yourself.

Ketogenic's is a high fat diet that will encourage the body to burn fat stores in your body. Yes, you heard that right, a high fat diet that will actually burn your existing fat. Sounds like a pretty good deal, but before you run out to the local Krispy Kreme and start scarfing down crullers in the name of ketogenic's, let's get a little background info first.

The ketogenic diet was developed in the 1920's as a potential treatment for epilepsy. The diet replaces carbohydrates with fat, because carbohydrates break down into glucose, which can trigger seizures in epileptics, while fat breaks down into fatty acids and ketone bodies, which are then used to replace glucose in the brain for energy. The diet lost its popularity with the advent of anticonvulsant drugs of the day. It jumped back onto the scene in the 1990's when the son of Jim Abrahams, a Hollywood producer, found relief for his epilepsy through this innovative diet approach. Now, more and more individuals are choosing ketogenic diets for their own weight loss goals.

Everyone is looking for a way to turn back the clock. To get that figure they had when they were in high school. Who would have thought the answer lie in high fat foods? It sees, however, that just may be the case. You see once the body begins to use fat as a source for energy rather than carbohydrates, your body has entered into the state of ketosis. In this state, you actually feel less hungry. The body using the fat as energy combined with your reduced appetite can result in quick and significant weight loss in the dieter. So, we are talking about replacing carbohydrates with fat, but what foods exactly will qualify for this type of enhanced food regimen?

The list of fatty foods is long and includes bacon, butter, mayonnaise, hot dogs, cream, nuts and more. While eating the fatty foods, you are trying to stay away from any of the carb loaded foods. The include almost anything made with sugar; cake, pie, cookies, candy and white flour foods as well including pasta and white bread. The diet sounds simple enough, but remember, this diet was developed by doctors to use as a treatment for patients with epilepsy. It was generally monitored by a doctor and it is recommended you heed similar advice. In our quest for a better body and fat loss, many of us will try anything. A ketogenic diet may well help you achieve your goals, but it can be risky as well. High blood pressure, high cholesterol and other medical conditions can occur while on a diet such as this. Combining the diet with a rigorous and consistent exercise routine will certainly help to limit the existence and severity of such conditions, but not avoid them completely. Be careful, do your research, and seek your doctor's advice whenever you are starting a modified diet or exercise plan.

Printed in Great Britain
by Amazon